AMSTERDAM ARCHITECTURE
1994-96

Amsterdam Architecture
1994-96

Edited by Maarten Kloos

ARCAM/Architectura & Natura Press

Editor
Maarten Kloos
Text editor and production
Birgitte de Maar
Translated by
Jane Zuyl-Moores
Copy editing
H.J. Scheepmaker
Design
Typography & Other Serious Matters
Printing
Drukkerij Rob Stolk, Amsterdam
Publisher
ARCAM, in conjunction with
Architectura & Natura Press, Amsterdam

ISBN 90 71570 51 7

*Published with the financial support of
the Dutch Ministry of Housing, Spatial Planning and Environment,
Intervam BML, Amsterdamse Aannemers Vereniging
and ARCAM's main sponsors*

CONTENTS

7   *Introduction*, Maarten Kloos

11   *A new appearance for Amsterdam*, Koos Bosma

43   *Selected projects*, Birgitte de Maar

44   Housing Haarlemmerbuurt, Claus & Kaan

46   Private house Prinseneiland, Tijmen Ploeg

48   N s traffic control building, N s Ingenieursbureau

50   Housing Witteneiland, Lafour & Wijk

52   De Kolk development, Van Berkel & Bos

55   *Squares*, Willem Koerse

58   Housing My Side, De Architekten Cie

60   Housing Quellijnstraat, Rowin Petersma

62   Housing Dapperbuurt, Hans van Heeswijk

64   Housing Wijttenbachstraat, Bart Duvekot

66   Housing Eerste van Swindenstraat, Tangram

69   *The street façade*, Vincent van Rossem

72   Office and information centre New Deal, Heren 5

74   Housing Vrolikstraat, Duinker, Van der Torre

76   Housing Vrolikstraat, Steigenga Smit

78   Housing Vespuccistraat, Meyer & Van Schooten

CONTENTS

80   Housing Skydome, Wiel Arets

83   *The circular building*, Bernard Hulsman

86   Dwellings and shops De Branding, De Architectengroep

88   Housing and mosque Insulindeweg, Duinker, Van der Torre

90   Children's day care centre JoJo, Architektengroep 69 Groenhout

92   Housing Beethovenstraat, Hans Bosch

94   Housing Victorieplein, Dobbelaar De Kovel De Vroom

97   *The programme*, Marinus Oostenbrink

100   Laboratory Anna's Hoeve, Benthem Crouwel

102   Dwellings and shops Osdorpplein, OD 205

104   Housing Gulden Kruis, Lafour & Wijk

106   Training centre De Toekomst, René van Zuuk

108   Tunnels and viaducts, Quist Wintermans

111   *The structural artwork*, Frederike Huygen

114   Housing Ookmeerweg, MVRDV

116   Housing Sloto, Fenna Oorthuys

118   Housing Eben, Edhoffer Van Exel

122   Housing Nieuw Sloten, De Architectengroep

124   Housing Nieuw Sloten, Sjoerd Soeters

126   Housing De Aker, Geurst & Schulze

129   *Remodelling the city*, Maarten Kloos

135   List of selected projects

141   Sources

INTRODUCTION

It cannot be denied: Amsterdam is a prosperous city, which is flourishing in many respects. The city's economic position is strong and tourism is booming. The urban renewal process has shifted from the centre via the nineteenth- and early-twentieth-century districts to the postwar expansion areas. Government and private enterprise have expressed their confidence in the city by investing a total of one billion guilders in the period 1991-95 in public space and shops in the city centre. Moreover, according to a recent report, residents are by and large extremely pleased with the living environment in the city's newest housing developments.

Architecturally and urbanistically, perhaps the city's most important feature is that it still has a recognizable identity. This is of course based on the architecture of several nineteenth-century architects, the Amsterdam School, H.P. Berlage and Functionalism. In the seventies and eighties, a highly distinctive if sometimes unspectacular urban regeneration was added to this. With regard to the most recent architecture, it is clear that Amsterdam is participating, albeit calmly, in the circus of international fashion. The most important styles, movements and trends are represented, and a number of (inter)national leading architects have been given the opportunity to build here. The architecture is, however, characterized by understatement and restraint.

This impression was reinforced in early 1997 when, for the second time, ARCAM asked a committee of experts to select a number of projects for a review of the best architecture built in Amsterdam over the past three years. This time the committee, which viewed more than 130 buildings and sites, comprised architectural historian Koos Bosma, architect Nan Raap and adviser on the visual arts and architecture Luce van Rooy.

It was noteworthy that the committee was unanimous in its preference for clarity and simplicity. This manifested itself in, among other things, a tendency to apply a range of criteria in different situations. All the buildings were evaluated in their context and, depending on the situation, a discreet and neutral character was rated as highly as flamboyance. Some projects have not been included although their quality is comparable to that of the buildings presented here. A choice had to be made and it is good to emphas-ize therefore that this book does not present a comprehensive overview of three years of building construction in Amsterdam.

Moreover, when discussing a certain period, it is necessary to draw boundary lines. In this case, two aspects have been taken into consideration: the buildings had to be completed by early 1997, and the committee had to be able to evaluate the projects in relation to their surroundings. This latter aspect was particularly relevant because large-scale, ambitious operations are actually being carried out in the city. The first components have been realized, but a grand statement is not yet discernible. For this reason it was decided that the housing projects on the G W L site (the former site of the municipal water board) and on Java-eiland should be looked at at a later date.

Outsiders will be surprised to find that certain projects have failed to stand the test of criticism. Some projects have not been included on grounds of architectural quality, even though they are well loved for other reasons. Major prestige projects such as the Rembrandt Tower (1995) and Arena Stadium (1996) are not discussed at length. And readers of the glossy architecture magazines will notice that the selection committee has not let itself be influenced by previous procedures. A project which won a prize in the Europan I competition has not been included in this book and some projects by major architects which, like all projects, were judged on their merits were found wanting.

The following text by committee member Koos Bosma is not a report of the evaluation process but it has of course been influenced by it. A number of subjects raised in committee discussions are dealt with here in separate essays. The authors are the philosopher Willem Koerse, the architectural historian Vincent van Rossem, architecture critic Bernard Hulsman, housing expert Marinus Oostenbrink and art historian Frederike Huygen.

MAARTEN KLOOS

Renewal
Bijlmermeer
[situation
1997]

A NEW APPEARANCE
FOR AMSTERDAM

Amsterdam's settlement pattern is changing at a rapid rate. Until well into the seventies, growth was regulated in accordance with the main lines laid down in the General Extension Plan of 1935. Put simply, this growth model comprised an autonomous city centre linked via arterial roads to the lobate expansion areas. This meant that attractive parts of the countryside could as it were penetrate the body of the city. The projected district of IJburg, an island town of 45,000 inhabitants in the IJmeer, can be regarded as the last lobate urban expansion. In accordance with a council decree of 4 September 1996, 18,000 dwellings are to be built here.

Meanwhile, the unbuilt space between the lobes has in many places been filled by small-scale housing projects and industrial parks. The extensive districts of Nieuw Sloten and Middelveldsche Akerpolder were even presented as widenings of the lobes. These lobes cannot, however, be endlessly stretched, because they are based on acceptable cycling and walking distances to green areas and to public transport stops. Moreover, the lobes owe their location to a specific relationship between variegated building development and agrarian landscapes. If all these landscapes are built on, the lobate structure will lose its meaning.

Regional developments · At a regional level, two urban corridors have been created in recent decades, namely Haarlem-Amsterdam and Schiphol-Het Gooi-Utrecht, in which new development is chiefly concentrated near green space facilities, traffic intersections and centres for public transport. This means that Amsterdam's familiar lobate system is being replaced by the planning of linear growth zones along the banks of the IJ and the so-called Zuid-as (south axis, the large arc which connects Schiphol Airport with the south and south-east of Amsterdam), in which traffic structures function as a carrier.

Attempts to unite the various projects along the south bank of the IJ, where former docklands are being urbanized, into a single scheme have after ten years ended in failure. This is why in recent years several peninsulas (KNSM-eiland, Java-eiland, and Borneo/Sporenburg) have been dealt with separately. The approach has proved effective.

The development of the Zuid-as was from the outset an unstoppable phenomenon. The location of this axis – close to Schiphol, the A 10 orbital motorway, and the major arterial routes to the east and south – attracted mainly companies. Firstly to the area Amstel 111, which borders on the last substantial urban expansion area in the tradition of the General Extension Plan, the Bijlmermeer (Amsterdam-Zuidoost, with 100,000 inhabitants), and later to other sites along the Zuid-as. Numerous large and flourishing companies left the city centre, partly because of its poor accessibility by car. Affluent citizens, owning one or more cars, sought refuge chiefly in the south-west of the city (Nieuw Sloten, Middelveldsche Akerpolder). The new central area around Arena Stadium has to be ready by the year 2000 in connection with the European football championship. This plan comprises, among other things, an extensive entertainment area and an office district. Parallel with this ambitious building project, a large-scale urban regeneration project is underway in the Bijlmermeer.

Generally speaking, the greater the distance between the expansion areas and the historical city centre, the lower the housing densities. The Oostelijk Haven-gebied (Eastern Docklands) has 100, IJburg 60 and Nieuw Sloten 25 dwellings per hectare. This explains much of the criticism frequently levelled at current low-rise projects: objections include the extensiveness of the development, the exclusive focus on housing, the large distance to the city centre and the lack of historical identity. Nevertheless, the advantages of such housing locations outweigh the disadvantages: witness the expansion of the municipalities around Amsterdam. The migration to these extensive suburbs has the character of a major exodus.

In order to counter this trend towards suburbanization, building densities around the city centre are being substantially increased, while preserving a high-quality living environment. In conjunction with this, enormous efforts are being directed to preserving well-designed facilities (such as large department stores) and to introducing traffic measures (underground and multi-storey car parks and parking regulations) in the city centre. A major problem, however, is the number of square metres per household. If Amsterdam were to fulfil the wishes of its citizens as regards living space the city would be twice its present size. The crucial question is, therefore, whether the historic city centre with its higher building densities will exercise a greater attraction than the regional suburbs with their extremely low densities.

Size and scale · Since the sixties there has been a strong opposition to any increase in scale in the vulnerable city centre. Citizens protested against the large and sometimes tall new buildings of banks and the university. The buildings which provoked the strongest reaction were the Nederlandsche Bank in Frederiksplein (M.F. Duintjer, 1968), which is hermetically sealed on the ground floor, and the Burgemeester Tellegenhuis, popularly known as the 'Maupoleum' (designed by Zanstra, Gmelig Meyling and De Clerq Zubli, 1971). To Amsterdammers, these buildings symbolized the penetration of corporate capital in the city.

The rehabilitation of the eastern part of the inner city was accompanied by an increase in scale along the axis Weesperstraat/Wibautstraat. This came to a temporary halt near Waterlooplein, the town hall/opera house and the Maupoleum. Because the area behind here was never adapted to the new scale, the latter building became a symbol of the arrested increase in scale of the seventies. Remarkably enough, it has now been demolished and replaced by an even larger volume. The new volume, which comprises the theatre school of the Amsterdamse Hogeschool voor de Kunsten and an office building (1997), is partly built on the existing foundations and underground car park of the old volume, but has been more successfully inserted in its surroundings; the street has been narrowed, the long building has been cut in two and the building height conforms to the neighbouring buildings.

This example shows that the city council is still intent on keeping major employers and functions which attract the public in the city centre. This is now possible because attitudes towards increase in scale have softened and because the new architecture, fashionable though it is, has a contemporary repertoire of forms which is more compatible with the surrounding historical structures.

On the whole, architects seek to conform their buildings, at least as regards appearance, to the size and scale of the city centre. Noteworthy, however, are the number of residential towers and office towers being erected in the old and new expansion areas and in the business parks, and which are visible from the city centre. For example, the tower of the Nederlandsche Bank has been reinforced by the Rembrandt Tower in the De Omval area (ZZ+P, 1995). What is striking is that this tower, like the most recent office towers on prime sites such as Arena Stadium, has little aesthetic appeal. It seems that, although the taboo on building tall towers was broken down in the nineties, architects

*Theatre
school,*
Teun
Koolhaas
Associates
[1997]

De Omval
[situation
1997]

still lack the skill necessary in order to produce architecturally successful towers. Furthermore, clients evidently do not consider the aesthetic quality of their towers to be important for their corporate identity. Which is why they are one-dimensional, no more than a landmark. This is a pity, because the towers are also an expression of the fact that Amsterdam – whose government is already decentralized – no longer has a single geographic and administrative centre; rather it has several centres. Each of these centres needs its own facilities, its own identifiable image and aura, because otherwise they become barren monocultures.

There are a number of reasons for the return of the residential tower in the streetscape. Sometimes the tower is integrated in the plan in order to achieve a higher dwelling density and to increase variation. Examples include the residential tower by Atelier Pro in Nieuw Sloten (1994) and the residential tower by Wiel Arets on KNSM-eiland (see pp. 80-81). The housing blocks by Cees Dam in the De Omval area are intended to give expression to the phenomenon of metropolitan living. The Hekla tower by Tangram in Middelveldsche Akerpolder (1995) and the Flevopark block by Hans Wagner, a raised residential tower with nine storeys built in 1995, mark the boundary of the city district in which they stand. All the residential towers built recently are, by and large, as regards their basic form, considerably more complex than their predecessors of the sixties. They have been constructed like a fan, a series of wedges, an oval or the segment of a circle. Moreover, the use of materials is much more interesting. Size is not usually a problem.

Mega-projects · Size and scale is a problem, however, in the case of Arena Stadium, a mega-project in Amsterdam-Zuidoost. The Arena, with its pitch ten metres above surface level, functions not only as the new stadium of Ajax football club, but also as a stage for major concerts. Typologically and architecturally the stadium has little to offer. The building looks like a mussel on a decorated socle. Like a solidified logistic programme, the building boasts a multi-storey car park (with space for 2,600 cars on two parking decks), infrastructural access (via a dual carriageway beneath the car park) and hideous barriers to control the crowds.

The problem outlined above is also evident in the area around the Arena, namely in the curved viaducts of the metro near Duivendrecht. The design of the seven-metre-high viaducts is lacklustre. Here too, there was an opportunity to make not only a logistic, but also a combined civil-engineering and architectural contribution to the area. And here too, the opportunity has been missed. It is worrying that, with so many projected infrastructural schemes, so many civil-engineering structures are being built which lack either a straightforward or a sophisticated design.

Fortunately, opposite the stadium and the viaducts stand other structures. The Ajax youth training centre (René van Zuuk, see pp. 106-7), for example, has much more to offer. The main stand, whose roof is suspended like an imposing arched bridge from the stays of two heavy, diagonally placed steel tubes, is an impressive structure. It does however distract the attention and in this respect the structure is perhaps too expressionistic. The main building of this training centre, on the other

Amsterdam Arena, Grabowsky & Poort [1996]

Metro viaducts, De Beer & Winnubst [1996]

hand, has great visual appeal. Here too, the construction serves the spaces it creates. But the meticulous detailing and use of materials, and the autonomy of materials and surfaces lend the spaces an enormous clarity.

Another successful structure is the cycle tunnel, designed by Quist Wintermans (see pp. 108-9), beneath a dual carriageway near Arena Stadium. The tunnel, which is extra wide, is daylit via gaps in the central reservation of the road above. In addition, there are gaps in the side walls through which light falls and which, together with the bright colours of the concrete, create startling effects. Architectural interventions such as this, which do not follow logically from the civil-engineering concept, provide more than public safety alone.

Large-scale housing projects · When evaluating recent housing projects the turnaround in national housing policy has to be taken into account: the reduction of social housing and the expansion of the market for affluent middle-class housing consumers. For privatization brought with it not only a different ideology, different power relations and a different financing system, but also different design concepts. In the sixties, social housing was above all aimed at teaching the masses bourgeois standards; in the seventies, it was characterized by participation, and in the eighties by outward show. Today, the citizen is the subject of study. Fashionable topics such as 'nomadism' and 'cocooning' dominate the discussion.

The housing developments propagated by the central government lack sociological aims. Instead, they slavishly follow market trends. As a result, these new districts are dominated by white middle-class families. Such urban expansion areas usually have an ambiguous infrastructural purpose: the dwelling has to be close to a motorway exit and at the same time optimally linked to public transport stops. Individualism predominates, and there is no pretence at communality. The only facilities in such districts are the shopping centre with car park, a snack bar and health club with gymnasium.

What is certain is that more than ever before supposed life styles are taken into account; life styles which require a particular architectural design. Furthermore, there is a trend towards a privatization centred on the intimacy of the family and this is manifest in architecture. In the suburbs, for example, two dwelling types which were never particularly popular this century are being revived: the drive-in dwelling and the patio dwelling. The drive-in dwelling, in which the car receives special attention, is built in extremely narrow residential streets. Its most important feature is that the front garden is sacrificed in order to create either a parking space for the car (see the car port in Koen van Velsen's project in Nieuw Sloten, 1995) or a ramp to the underground built-in garage beneath a living floor which is situated at a slightly higher level (see, for example, the dwellings by Duinker, Van der Torre in Nieuw Sloten, 1996). This type permits variations of floor plans and ceiling heights.

The patio dwelling, in which extra private space is created, is a Mediterranean dwelling type in origin. Here, the open inner court, which is a social space,

*Drive-in
dwellings,
Nieuw Sloten,*
Duinker,
Van der Torre
[1996]

*Patio
dwellings,
De Aker,*
Van Sambeek
Van Veen
[1996]

allows users to be in the open air and yet at the same time they are protected from the strong sunlight. Characteristic of these times is that in the Netherlands this dwelling type is used in a completely different context, namely there where high dwelling densities are required together with maximum privacy and optimal sunlighting. With this type, back-to-back dwellings are possible (see the patio houses by Sambeek & Van Veen in De Aker, the western part of Middelveldsche Akerpolder, realized 1994-97). The major drawback of the patio type, however, is that, if space is extremely limited, living becomes introverted and occupants are visually confined in their cells, taking a breath of air at regular times in their private light court. This trend towards privatization therefore needs questioning.

Although they cherish their individualism, the great majority of Amsterdammers are very conventional in their choice of dwelling type. Most, it seems, have a preference for a single-family house with garden in a suburb with considerable shopping facilities and other amenities. They are lured to bleak neighbourhoods with terraced houses where they get up to their ears in debt. Few Amsterdammers deviate from this norm. It is difficult to quantify how many people would choose to live in a fundamentally different way if suitable alternatives were available. This is an important observation because all sorts of assertions are being made about life styles which, given the increasing privatization, need to be taken into account in housing. The problem is, however, that a certain life style is not linked to a particular dwelling type or a clearly defined architectural design. In that respect architects have little use for sociological speculations. What is more important is that architecture does not impede a particular (standardized) life style.

Vacant sites · When we follow the chronology of new housing projects on vacant sites, then the developments outlined above are visible in the urban design plan of these districts. The housing in IJ-Plein in Amsterdam-Noord (1980-87), designed under the supervision of Rem Koolhaas and his Office for Metropolitan Architecture, was social democracy's final attempt to develop a waterfront in a former docklands area for Amsterdammers with a lower than average income. The open row housing, inspired by housing of the twenties, has been situated on the site in such a way that light, air and greenery have been democratically divided among all the dwellings, with the result, incidentally, that no one gets very much of anything.

The antipode of the flirtation with the architecture of the historical avant-garde is the urban design plan by Jo Coenen for KNSM-eiland (1988). Coenen's design harks back to the perimeter block clad with brick and endeavours to find a link with the design principles of the classical city. The rather static design, in which public space is scarce, is interesting for the deviations from the unambiguous concept: the complex pleated building by Kollhoff & Rapp (1993-94) and the residential tower by Wiel Arets.

Java-eiland (now under construction), which is a continuation of KNSM-eiland, is based on yet another

Housing Java-eiland, north façade [situation 1997]

*Housing
Java-eiland,*
Jo Crepain
[1996]

concept. In Coenen's plan, social housing was dominant and, moreover, was built on the south side of the
island. In the design by Sjoerd Soeters for Java-eiland
(1990) the new market relations are manifest. The
basic structure is a system of canals at right angles to the
length of the island. As a result, there are no really long
building blocks. The high buildings have been conceived as an assemblage of individualized façades, as in
the ring of canals in Amsterdam's city centre. Soeters
has created dwelling differentiation by engaging a
number of architects to design the façades, with the
emphasis on cacophony. At the same time he has
ensured a certain unity by prescribing the building
height and by repeating the façades of the various
architects in other blocks. In comparison with the long,
static and horizontal blocks on KNSM-eiland, the
development on Java-eiland is vertical and varied.

The urban design plan for Borneo/Sporenburg,
designed by Adriaan Geuze of West 8 (1993), can be

Urban plan Borneo/ Sporenburg, West 8 [1993]

seen as a reaction to the profusion of images in the new residential districts of recent decades. The problem with these neighbourhoods is that variation has become an end in itself and has not developed from design principles, nor is it a deviation from these principles. Geuze was even stricter than Coenen in laying down the main lines of the urban structure for Borneo/Sporenburg. He chose, in conformity with market demands, low-rise housing with the front door on the street.

As a result, half of the plots have been built with short rows of three storeys with numerous possibilities for variation. The area of low-rise has been deliberately interrupted in three places by high-rise buildings of 8 to 14 storeys. The assemblage of narrow plots, at right angles to the quays, is punctuated here and there by alleys. The streets are narrow because residents have to park on their property. This has the effect of emphasizing the elongated form of the peninsula and means that

GWL *site*
[situation
1997]

there is no public space. Evidently, the quay and the water are deemed sufficient. The high density (100 dwellings per hectare) results in an introverted dwelling type. Each dwelling has a roof terrace and its own interior space in the form of a patio. The district is still under construction, so it is not yet possible to give an evaluation of its quality.

On the edge of Staatsliedenbuurt, on the GWL site, another interesting neighbourhood (600 dwellings) is under construction. The plan, by Kees Christiaanse (1993), is environmentally friendly and car-free, so that here too, a density of 100 dwellings per hectare was possible. The composition consists of an assemblage of architectural objects on a green surface with long sightlines. Situated next to the preserved water tower and pumping station are short rows of five storeys in red brick. The site is screened off by an extremely elongated building block which rises from four to nine storeys. The crucial question with regard to this neighbourhood is whether residents, walkers and cyclists will want or be able to comply with the code of behaviour of this restrictive environment.

Expansion areas · In addition to new developments on vacant sites in the city centre, traditional expansion areas are also of course built on the periphery. After the Bijlmermeer, Nieuw Sloten is the first major expansion area in Amsterdam (5,000 dwellings, realized in the period 1988-96). Point of departure was a high dwelling density in low-rise development. In the original plan, the city's planning department had divided the area into a grid of plots. This system was then undermined by the introduction of an access system in the form of a tuning fork (north-south) which is bisected by an east-west tram line, cutting the district in two. Along one side of the tram line a centre has been built with residential blocks, offices and shops. Though centrally situated, this centre is completely isolated by the roads and the tram line. Around it are a series of low-rise neighbourhoods. The irregularities in the land division, which are the result of the traffic system, have been filled with parks and green facilities.

The architecture of Nieuw Sloten is extremely heterogeneous. This was partly due to the fragmented planning process (among other things, the supervisor was replaced) which preceded the architectural design. Three interesting projects have been executed over the past three years. By way of compensation for the traditional dominance of male architects, a number of women architects were invited to develop market-sector housing on eight islands. These islands are situated on the periphery, literally in the margin of Nieuw Sloten. Although one has reservations about such patchwork development, the architecture which has been realized is of a high quality (see pp. 116-19). In the midst of the cacophony of forced variation, the neighbourhood designed by Hans Ruijssenaars is like a breath of fresh air (see pp. 122-23). He has created coherence by using one dominant colour (white), by clearly demarcating public and private areas, and by 'edging' the architectural units. The underlying idea was, given the extreme privatization behind the front door, to create a sense of community in an area which evokes associations with a communal courtyard.

The most striking element in Nieuw Sloten is the housing project designed by Sjoerd Soeters (see pp. 124-25). This small neighbourhood of 156 dwellings lies between an area of open row housing and an indeterminate residual area with a narrow golden edge. All the streets have an identical curvature, which meant that the plan could be filled with two dwelling types. The roofs of the dwellings at the head ends on the water side are clad with aluminium panels which are terminated near the eaves by a white perforated collar, reminiscent of the traditional caps worn in the province of Zeeland. One can of course object to such literal references, which, incidentally, are the rule rather than the exception in Soeters' work. The fact is, however, that here the reference is restrained and effective and is not tedious. The small neighbourhood is terminated on the water side by six free-standing blocks with 'Zeeland' caps without collar, which are not, as is often the case, crammed together, but stand separate in space.

De Aker lies in a former market-gardening area which is directly linked to Nieuw Sloten and Osdorp. The polder's existing waterways, dikes and ribbons of development have been preserved. The main roads are wide and thickly planted. Together with the drainage channels and the central square, which has yet to be constructed, these elements structure the district. The entrance to the district is marked by a tall residential tower. The aim was to give each neighbourhood its own identity. A great deal of attention has been paid to the public space by constructing 'green courts', drainage channels, bridges, a meadow area and avenues which link up to the main roads. When completed, this residential area (3,500 dwellings) will be imbedded in a decor of green space, water and dikes. Contrasting with this attempt at enriching and integrating the existing structures is the dull architectural design realized to date. Practically none of the architects have been inspired to produce anything of note here.

Generations of architects · The depression in architectural training which began in the seventies, a period in which achieving social objects was considered more important than producing high-quality architecture, seems to be over. The first generation to get back on its feet, now aged between 45 and 60, can on the whole be numbered among the neomodernists who seek to revive and rework the original repertoire of forms of the historical avant-garde of the twenties. Of primary importance for the neomodernists was the honest relationship between interior and exterior. In addition, the expression of the constructional principle was for them

the essence of architecture. This puritanical trend was later moderated by a certain Mediterraneanization; for example, the use of stuccoed façades in pastel shades characteristic of Italian and Spanish architecture.

The group of architects which at the moment determines Amsterdam's architectural signature can be regarded as the second generation, which once again aspires to a superior architectural quality. For this second generation, now aged between 30 and 45, architecture has a different essence. While preserving the qualities of the floor plan, the expression of the building type and the materialization of everyday ornament (the façade and the roof form) are considered to be the most important contributions to public space. It is noteworthy that traditional building materials, which for decades were neglected, such as brick and wood are once again extremely popular and are employed in a wide variety of ways. The fact that the taboo on the pitched roof has been raised is surely also due to the typically Dutch instruments of control such as the building inspectorate and the city-image plan. Furthermore, there is the national *Bouwbesluit 1992*, which with its regulations regarding environmental friendliness and heat and sound insulation influences the appearance of the dwelling. Last but not least, there is the influence of the architecture of other countries, images of which reach the Netherlands via architecture magazines. Taste has undeniably changed, as a result of which a new mix of Dutch tradition and international glamour has come into being.

De Aker, under construction [situation 1997]

The new architectural principles are able to flourish thanks to changes in the commissions situation. In the eighties, rented dwellings comprised ninety per cent of housing production; this is now thirty per cent. The housing corporations, which previously served the rented sector with money borrowed from the government, are increasingly playing the role of real-estate investor and risk-bearing property developer. As a result, attention has shifted to the up-market, tax-subsidized private dwelling. The boarding house, the temporary residence of the cosmopolitan, the student, the correspondent or the homeless, is no longer the object of architectural creativity. The era of inexpensive housing for the lowest incomes and cultural minorities seems to have come to an end. For these groups, moving up the housing ladder means moving into the dwellings previously occupied by the affluent middle classes who have now relocated to the new suburbs.

Architecture · The architects of the second generation have an enormous repertoire of plot divisions, types of access, typologies and floor plans. They are constantly looking at each other's projects and seem to be trying to outdo each other with new ideas. In order to keep up with the latest trends, and in the hope of being able to cash in on the glamour of the international architecture scene, extreme experiments with form are not eschewed. Nevertheless, architects are not indifferent to flexible living programmes or social issues. When asked, they produce dwellings with flexible floor plans suitable for a variety of modes of living, combined with home office if desired. For example,

*Housing
Ookmeerweg,*
MVRDV
[1996-97]

elderly people who are looking for a smaller dwelling can have all their requirements fulfilled, even when they are housed in a contemporary 'residential colony'. The most bizarre project in this respect is a so-called 'residential care complex' in Osdorp, designed by the youngest members of the second generation (MVRDV, 1996/97; see pp. 114-15).

In the past, the elderly were housed in buildings typologically related to the hotel and the hospital. They had 40 square metres of living space, a minimum which has now been increased to 75 square metres. In Osdorp the architects have opted for an extreme solution, inspired by the apartment block in Sittard (1995) by their contemporary Willem Jan Neutelings. This building comprises a set-back base (yellow), a box with apartments (black) and 'roof villas' clad with wood on two storeys, some of which are set back and some of which project. The building has been given sculptural expression by contrasting the three storeys as regards form and use of materials. M V R D V has taken this principle of contrast to an extreme.

Because the building height and sunlighting regulations meant that only 87 of the 100 apartments required could be housed in the gallery flat, the remaining 13 apartments have been housed in four boxes, clad with overlapping wooden strips, which project from the façade. The boxes are as wide as the gallery flat itself and seem to defy the laws of gravity, as a result of which the building seems menacing. The other side of the building is just as striking. Like the drawers of a cupboard which has fallen over, 87 balconies project from the façade in an irregular pattern. The sizes of the windows vary enormously. This quirkiness and the dark-glazed balcony balustrades lend the projecting private terrace an amusing quality. It seems to be a parody of the balcony euphoria of the seventies and eighties. It is perhaps characteristic of these times that architectural experiments are being carried out precisely there where a future social problem is looming. In our youthful society, the age at which people acquire the status of old-age pensioner is constantly being lowered. This category of senior citizens is as a rule affluent, which is why they are offered a serious architectural living environment.

Street façades · The urban regeneration of the inner city is now in its final phase. Numerous small infill projects (social housing) have been completed in Dapperbuurt and Indische Buurt. These projects show a variety of approaches. Examples of autonomous infills can be seen in Dapperstraat and surroundings: the grey curtain walls designed by Hans van Heeswijk, behind which are a wide variety of floor plans (see pp. 62-63). Contrasting with these autonomous façades is the elimination of the façade in the frontage of a project in Vespuccistraat, designed by Meyer & Van Schooten (see pp. 78-79). Between two towers in red brick, which house the stairwells, is a grid of steel beams. The entire façade space is set back more than two metres and is clad with corrugated sheets. The stratification is for giving occupants south-facing exterior space (balconies or glazed sun lounges). The block in the side street has been designed to contrast with this façade with screen. Here, a glazed façade conceals the dwelling typology. The semi-transparent glass sheets the size of a paving stone create a fascinating stratification of colours and reflections.

A similar contrast in approach can be seen in the street façades by the architectural practices Steigenga Smit and Duinker, Van der Torre. In Vrolikstraat, Steigenga Smit have replicated the nineteenth-century composition and texture of the closed street façade, and have even bevelled the edge of the block in order to adapt it to the lower buildings in a side street. Living space and work space have been created in the basement. The spectacular contemporary façade with roof terraces, balconies and glazed stairwells is situated at the rear of the building block (see pp. 76-77). In the projects by Duinker, Van der Torre, the circulation points and the exterior space are usually situated on the street side. The introduction of small blocks with individual dwellings disturbs the homogeneity of the existing street façade. Most of the time, it is therefore necessary to make the façade composition autonomous by means of a framework, within which numerous variants can be created. This sidesteps the problem of fitting the façade into its context, although sometimes, despite adaptation in the form of plinth and cornice line, this gives rise to a fragmented street frontage.

Another problem arises in the case of infills in a context for which the historic preservation department sets limiting conditions. Here too, extremes occur. The architectural office Claus & Kaan was commissioned to house three dwellings (social housing) in a historic building in Haarlemmerbuurt (see pp. 44-45). Next to the existing monument they built a glazed structure which is radically simple and virtually devoid of detailing. Because the floor space per storey was extremely limited, the architects have linked the buildings to form a single organizational unit. The infill functions as a 'drip' and houses the access, sanitary facilities and the bedrooms of the dwellings.

The De Kolk project (see pp. 52-53) shows a very different, more subtle approach. Here, instead of working with contrasts, the possibilities of historical references have been exploited to the full. Designed by the architectural practice Van Berkel & Bos, De Kolk is undoubtedly the most complex project of recent years. The programme comprised a hotel with 200 rooms, an underground car park, 6,000 square metres of shops on two storeys, 31 dwellings and an office. Furthermore, a number of old, listed façades had to be preserved. All these elements have been inserted in a structure with

De Kolk, Van Berkel & Bos [1996]

small streets and alleys. One of these alleys even functions as the plan's axis. The essence of the architectural
concept is the desire to make the project appear much
smaller than it really is. Only underground, in the car
park, is the size of the project clearly visible. The above-
ground elements of the programme are autonomous,
witness the series of disparate long and short façades.
When seen from a great distance, the different segments
form a single silhouette and it is possible to grasp the
scale of the conglomeration.

The architecture conforms to the historical surroundings through an idiosyncratic interpretation of
the existing façades. Van Berkel & Bos seek a special
way of referring to the historical surroundings by
means of the division of surfaces and use of material.
However, attention has been focused primarily on the
exterior and, partly because of a certain material fetish-
ism, the interior spaces lack a fitting design. In order to
knit the complex into the existing structure of alleys,
Van Berkel & Bos have articulated the prefabricated
façades so that there is no standpoint from where the
end of an alley can be seen. Nor can façades be viewed
frontally. The façades of the shopping arcade, the hotel
and the office, which are visible, have each been given
its own distinctive design to contrast with the neighbouring buildings. The architecture borrows elements
from its surroundings, and the façades have been treated almost graphically, with stepped, oblique and undu-
lating line segments. Once again, Van Berkel & Bos
have shown themselves to be diamond cutters who
have achieved a high degree of perfection and are
always seeking new effects.

The future · The city's large-scale expansion projects are almost complete. Within the municipal boundaries, new residential sites are available only in Amsterdam-Noord and along the banks of the IJ. If we assume that housing consumers consider the living environment to be more important than the distance they have to travel to work, then it is obvious that the few remaining areas of countryside and green structures will be defended come what may, and that the suburbs will be provided with high-quality facilities, with the emphasis on urban comfort, agrarian romanticism, and certainly high-quality architecture.

New office sites and business parks are still available along the Zuid-as. The direction in which the colonization of this axis will develop depends on, among other things, Schiphol's choice of site for expansion. The construction of the airport's fifth and sixth runways in Haarlemmermeer will have a different effect from expansion in the North Sea or in Markermeer near Lelystad, or even a gradual relocation of the airport to a completely new IJsselmeerpolder, the Markerwaard.

In any event, in view of the chronic lack of space, a contemporary form of government and an increase of Amsterdam's territory are inevitable. This cannot be interpreted as expansionism. The disintegration of the functional richness of the historic city centre, the emergence of autonomous subcentres, and the exodus to outlying municipalities can be seen as a farewell to the lobate city. This is being replaced by a multicore regional city, with a seemingly capricious settlement pattern; a city without an unequivocal centre, but with numerous more or less functionally specialized sectors, networks and nodes. There is a great need not only for a suitable regional administrative structure, but also for regional concepts which can shape the transformation which Amsterdam is currently undergoing. Such concepts take the present reality as a point of departure.

The focus is thus no longer on the myth of the old city, but rather on the new centres, the infrastructure, the landscape and the network nodes. Such a conceptual framework must not only contain a spatial idea which directs the main lines of the transformation, it must also create a spatial image which can anchor itself in the minds of citizens. If old Amsterdam wants to survive and remain economically resilient, then new Amsterdam will have to be designed with conviction.

KOOS BOSMA

SELECTED PROJECTS

The following selection of 31 projects realized in Amsterdam in the period 1994-96 concerns architectural objects which are also presented as such. This is possible because they are autonomous projects and, for example, a housing scheme on one side of the city is scarcely connected with an office building on the other side. Nevertheless, all of the projects are part of the same architectural and urbanistic culture. This is immediately apparent where clusters of projects have automatically come into being. Six essays discuss such pre-eminently urban themes as the square and the street façade, the significance of the structural artwork for the city and the circular building, as well as more hidden aspects such as the programme and the process of remodelling based on existing structures.

PROJECT DESCRIPTIONS BY

BIRGITTE DE MAAR

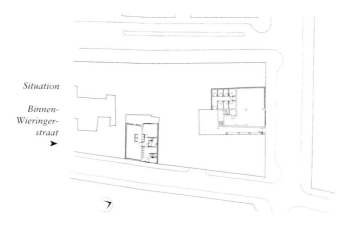

Situation

*Binnen-
Wieringer-
straat*

➤

*10 dwellings and commercial space, Haarlemmerstraat,
Binnenwieringerstraat* (Claus & Kaan Architecten, 1995)

This project for two locations in Haarlemmerbuurt involved the restoration of historic buildings and the infilling of small gaps. In Binnenwieringerstraat were two adjacent buildings, one of which was to be preserved and the other demolished. Because these are small plots and the floor area per storey is extremely small, the two buildings have been functionally interconnected and the apartments arranged horizontally over them. The infill contains functions such as access, sanitary facilities and kitchens. The living-rooms are situated in the old building.

The second site involved three buildings on either side of the corner of Haarlemmerstraat/Herenmarkt. In Haarlemmerstraat, one was restored and one was demolished and replaced by a new building. Because it is a defining feature of the street, the façade on Herenmarkt was first demolished and then reconstructed in front of the new building. Most of the entrances to the dwellings have been moved to the rear of the building. There is a traditional separation of functions in the building in Haarlemmerstraat: a shop on the ground floor, above which are various dwellings crowned by a maisonette.

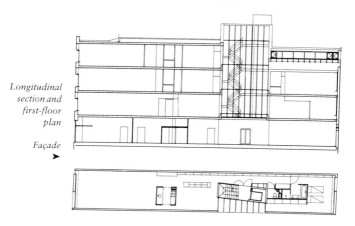

*Longitudinal
section and
first-floor
plan*

Façade

➤

Private house, Prinseneiland (Tijmen Ploeg, 1994)

In 1993, Tijmen Ploeg made a preliminary design for a private house on Prinseneiland, to replace an existing building with weak foundations. He based his design on the original building, with a front part comprising four storeys and a rear part comprising three storeys, separated by two light courts. During the drafting phase it became clear who was to occupy the house. These occupants – a group comprising three households – specified that the entire house be accessible with a lift and that there should be various communal facilities. These requirements formed the basis of the final design. The entire plot (35 metres deep, 5 metres wide) has been filled with a building whose front and rear parts are separated by a single light court. The storey height is the same as that of the neighbouring buildings, 2.90 metres. The ground floor houses a studio and communal facilities such as a garage, launderette and storage space. The first floor comprises a three-roomed apartment. On the second floor, a two-roomed apartment is situated in the front part of the house, combined with a work space at the rear. On the third floor is a two-roomed apartment linked to the group's guest accommodation, complete with kitchen unit and bathroom.

46

*Façade
De Ruyter-
kade*

NS *traffic control building and technical centre, De Ruyterkade*
(NS Ingenieursbureau – project architect Rob Steenhuis, 1994)

The traffic control building of the Dutch rail company NS is situated on a triangular strip along the railway line to the west of Amsterdam Centraal Station. This is the control centre for trains in the Amsterdam area. Security was therefore of paramount importance. Furthermore, the city council stipulated that the building, which is situated on a key site on the IJ in the city centre, should have a representative aura.

The result is a building which consists of three parts, each with its own function and each with a different basic form. The lower storey is a dark grey triangle. This contains at the front the main entrance. At the back, the triangle extends into the sharp angle between the diverging railway tracks. Here are the workshops, depots and changing rooms. The triangle supports a terracotta-coloured rectangular volume. This volume has three storeys and contains offices. The circular control room is separate from the office block. It rests on concrete cylinders which house the lift and staircases. The high room, with a diameter of 37 metres and a maximum height of 8 metres, has windows all round it. The circular roof is clad with copper which will eventually turn green.

Façade Wittenkade

216 dwellings and underground car park, Witteneiland
(Architektenburo L. Lafour & R. Wijk, 1996)

Lafour & Wijk designed 216 dwellings for Witteneiland on a triangular piece of land between Kostverlorenvaart, Kattensloot and Tweede Nassaustraat. The brief specified that the quays should remain public, that the new development be transparent with a variation in building heights and that it should accentuate the island character.

The dwellings are contained in five blocks. On the north-eastern side, the blocks fit in with the existing structure of perimeter blocks. These blocks are four and five storeys high and as regards size and material conform to the existing buildings. The exterior spaces of the dwellings are inside the frontage line. In the perimeter block are openings which afford a view of the inner garden and two monuments: the Nassaukerk and the 'Witte Huisje' (white house). Further towards the head of the peninsula the new development is more transparent. Here, the blocks stand separate in open green space. These are short blocks of gallery flats, seven and eight storeys high, with at the head end dwellings which have been turned round ninety degrees. Concrete bay windows reinforce the fanning-out effect of these free-standing blocks.

Free-standing blocks

Situation

Façade
Nieuwezijds
Voorburgwal

Car park, offices, hotel, 38 apartments, shops and cafés,

Nieuwezijds Kolk (Van Berkel & Bos Architectuurbureau, 1996)
The De Kolk project is situated in the heart of Amsterdam's old city centre, with its medieval street pattern. The complex is contained in three building blocks which are separated by the existing alleys. The first block is an office building in the sharp corner between Nieuwezijds Kolk and Nieuwezijds Voorburgwal. The other two blocks house shops and cafés and restaurants on the ground floor and the first floor. These functions are accessed via an entrance on Nieuwendijk. The hotel, which is situated above the shops, has 235 rooms on four floors and is accessed via an entrance on Nieuwezijds Kolk. The dwellings (part new-build, part renovation) are situated on the edges of the block and above the shops. The various functions within the complex have been expressed in the façades by giving each function its own aura. In order to fit the complex into its historic surroundings, aspects of the surrounding façades have been employed; for example, the strong vertical articulation and the visual distinction between ground floor and upper storeys. The façades consist of prefabricated concrete, bricks in various colours in vertical tile bonding, wood, and agglutinated glass in different hues.

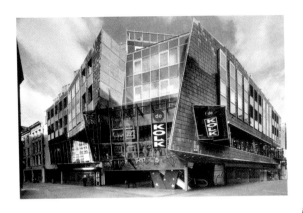

*Façade
Nieuwendijk*

*First-floor
plan*

Maria
Heinekenplein
[De Jong
Hoogveld
De Kat,
1995]

There is a great deal to say about squares. For the traveller, it is often the case that he or she does not know a city until he or she has visited its squares. Literature contains innumerable exemplary descriptions, and a survey of the historical events which squares have witnessed would fill several volumes. Nevertheless, one can ask oneself: what exactly is a square?

According to the dictionary, 'an open area surrounded by buildings'. Is a more basic, meagre definition possible? It is not of course incorrect, but it omits just about everything we imagine when we think of a square. We can advance the bold proposition that a square is not made, it comes into being, even though it is a well-known fact that many magnificent squares (some of which are urbanistic gems) have been designed. The solution to this paradox lies in whether or not a square is used by a community. Only when we 'take possession' of an open area does it acquire the character of a square. That is to say, a square is not only a spatial phenomenon, it is also a social phenomenon.

Research has shown that a square's form is not that relevant. Camillo Sitte and Rob Krier, both of whom developed principles whereby a space can become a square, have shown moreover that you can always find a square which differs in shape from all other squares. There are thus two aspects to this. While on the one hand design (size, scale) is undeniably important, this is clearly not a prerequisite for a vibrant square. In her classic book *The Death and Life of Great American Cities* (1965), Jane Jacobs describes four identical squares, only one of which, however, is used by the local community; the other three are dead, deserted spaces. It reminds me of the remarkable similarity between the Dutch new town Lelystad and the Italian town of Siena. It is said that Lelystad will never have a real centre because the central space is the result of the merging of the outskirts of three districts with a village character. But this is also true of Siena's famous Piazza del Campo.

If we look around us in Amsterdam we have to conclude that this city, which has a worthy tradition in urban design, has no splendid squares. If we restrict ourselves to the twentieth century then we can include H.P. Berlage's Plan Zuid with its wonderful street patterns and, indeed, here and there a square. This brings to mind an observation by the architectural historian Manfred Bock regarding Sitte and Berlage: whereas Sitte created public space (including squares) by means of architecture, Berlage needed public space as a context for architecture – an interesting contrast, which could point to the fact that the Netherlands has no tradition of designing squares to speak of.

Evidently, the Dutch still have difficulty designing squares. One of Berlage's squares (Mercatorplein in Amsterdam-West) is being reconstructed, and the way in which this is being done gives no cause for optimism. To be sure, the walls and the two towers have been carefully reconstructed (all credit to Berlage thus), but the unique element, the double kink in the through road, has been removed. As a result, the restful symmetry has also disappeared.

In addition to the reconstruction of existing squares, occasionally new squares are built in Amsterdam; for example, Maria Heinekenplein and Max Euweplein. Maria Heinekenplein is a space which has been reclaimed from the dense pattern of the nineteenth-century ring. This was possible because an old industrial building (part of the former Heineken brewery – hence the name) had been demolished. This genesis leads one to suspect that the square has not been designed as such but is really a residual space which is now called a square. Despite a rather bold intervention – the introduction of a dominant circular platform – this can be inferred from the space. Although Max Euweplein is also situated on a site formerly occupied by a building (a prison), it has been carefully designed as a square.

A comparison of the two squares points up the importance of the functions in the walls of a square. These functions, of course, attract people to a square and cause them to linger there. In Max Euweplein are shops, a kiosk which (very important) is open at night, and a café-restaurant. Moreover the square gives access to a casino. As a result, the square is fairly harmonious. Maria Heinekenplein lacks harmony, partly because the shops do not seem to belong to it.

As regards routing too, the two squares are very different. Whereas Maria Heinekenplein looks like an accidental left-over space next to a busy shopping street, Max Euweplein is a connecting element between the centre (Leidsestraat and Leidseplein) and Vondelpark and the P.C. Hooftstraat/Van Baerlestraat shopping area.

Another interesting case is a recently designed square in a purely residential area, Indische Buurt in Amsterdam-Oost. This fact alone makes it different from the squares described above. The designers of Makassarplein were given the opportunity to create a truly 'urban interior', and they have really gone to town. Differences in levels have been created, various types of paving have been laid and numerous objects have been erected, including a number of sculptures borrowed from Gaudi's Park Güell, Stonehenge-like monoliths and an assemblage of objects for children to play with.

The square is completely surrounded by buildings and is thus rather hidden, but that does not matter. It functions almost exclusively for the neighbourhood with its large immigrant families. It is important therefore when considering the social aspect of a square and the 'taking possession' of a space to make a distinction between squares in city centres (to which 'people' go and where the square fulfils an anonymous social function) and squares situated in residential areas.

Setting aside the need to make squares as 'play areas', such as Makassarplein, it seems to me that squares in residential districts have an uncertain future. Whether we like it or not, the individualization of society is a fact. This means, among other things, that there is rarely any commitment to the communal exterior space. And where there is no such commitment, the expression 'fear of open spaces' takes on a new meaning.

WILLEM KOERSE

North façade

'My Side', 106 dwellings, Veemkade (De Architekten Cie. – project architect: Frits van Dongen, 1995)

Frits van Dongen has housed 106 dwellings in two symmetrical blocks on the IJ. The orientation – to the IJ and the IJ harbour in the north, and to the city in the south – has determined the appearance of the buildings, the type of access and the dwelling types. On the water side, the buildings present themselves as a unit. The façade elements are of various materials such as glass, stucco and corrugated sheets. As a result, the interrelationship is clearly visible from the water. On the side of Oostelijke Handelskade, the appearance of the façades is determined by balconies, terraces and the wooden cladding of the top two stories, which makes this façade livelier.

In order to exploit the orientation to the full, all the dwellings have an open floor plan, and walls on the residential storeys have been kept to a minimum so as not to obstruct the view on either side. Situated directly on top of the car park, which is partly underground, are maisonettes with a void. The storeys above contain maisonettes of one and a half floors with corridor access. On the top storeys are smaller maisonettes with a large terrace.

*South façade
and
cross-section*

Entrance hall

31 dwellings, Quellijnstraat (Rowin Petersma, in collaboration with Liesbeth van der Pol, 1996)

At the end of 1993, Rowin Petersma received a commission for an infill project in Quellijnstraat in De Pijp, a nineteenth-century neighbourhood. The front of the site is situated on a small square with at the back a large and deep plot. The brief specified two-, three- and four-roomed flats which could be adapted to house the elderly. The prospective occupants had requested spaces for communal activities and this was the point of departure for the entire design. The entrance hall plays a central role and is designed as a meeting place. This high, glass atrium affords a view of both the small square at the front and the garden at the back, and so forms the transition between these two spaces. The materials used in the hall, such as paving stones, unprocessed wood and a blue ceiling, reinforce the character of a public space.

The dwellings on the ground floor are accessed directly from the street, the rest are accessed via galleries. These galleries are wider near the kitchens and the entrances to the dwellings. This creates an exterior space near each dwelling which encourages social contact. In addition, each dwelling has an exterior space in the form of a closable loggia.

Façade

Situation

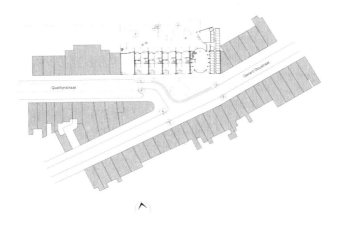

Von Zesen-straat

53 dwellings, Dapperstraat, Commelinstraat, Linnaeusstraat, Von Zesenstraat (Hans van Heeswijk, 1995)

This housing scheme comprises three blocks situated close together in Dapperbuurt. One of Van Heeswijk's aims was to show that the technical level of the façade as it seems to be the norm in office construction is also realizable in housing. He therefore employed the mode of construction, building components, detailing, materials and building method used in commercial and industrial buildings. Characteristics of Amsterdam's architecture have also been incorporated. This architecture is characterized by the closed block, the distinction between ground floor and upper storeys and between façades and side walls, a more or less flat façade and a strong vertical articulation which is usually based on the width of the plots. Although each of the three blocks has its own character, they present a uniform appearance. For example, the various dwelling types lie behind taut façades and the block sections are linked by means of transparent glass lifts and stairwells. A characteristic element is the round balcony with perforated steel. The grey façades clad with aluminium are decorated with colourful signs designed by R. Oxenaar and texts by the Dutch writers J.C. Bloem and Nescio.

Dapperstraat and Linnaeus- straat

Wijttenbach-straat

36 dwellings and commercial space, Dapperstraat,
Wijttenbachstraat (Bart Duvekot, 1995)

Duvekot was first commissioned to draw up a memorandum of design principles for Wijttenbachstraat. The most important features of the site incorporated in this memorandum are to be found in his design for the neighbourhood. For example, the vertical articulation, preservation of the building line, the accentuation of corner solutions and oriels, and an extra high ground-floor storey. The project consists of two parts. The block on the corner of Wijttenbachstraat and Dapperstraat has exuberant orange-red plasterwork, pillars and staggered corner windows. The façade on Dapperstraat is varied due to the different façade openings and the variety of materials used. The dwellings are mainly maisonettes with voids. The ground floor on Dapperstraat contains small studios. The dwellings above are accessed via a central stairwell.

At the beginning of Wijttenbachstraat is a small block of 12 dwellings. These dwellings are narrow and have been realized as maisonettes on one and a half or two floors. In both blocks, the storage spaces are situated in the basement on the garden side. As a result, there are no blind sections of façade on the street.

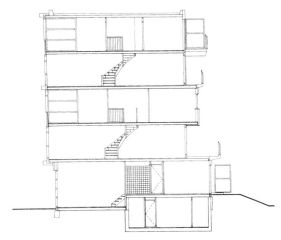

Façade and cross-section housing Dapperstraat/ Wijttenbach-straat

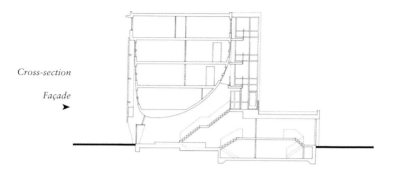

Cross-section

Façade

➤

79 dwellings and 15 shops, Eerste van Swindenstraat
(Tangram Architekten, 1996)

Tangram initially received a commission to design three blocks in Eerste van Swindenstraat, an important shopping street in Amsterdam-Oost. Later, another client asked them to design a fourth block, which meant that they could develop a new street façade with a total length of approximately 200 metres.

For all the blocks, the brief specified shops on the ground floor with above four storeys of subsidized dwellings. In order to give the shops the desired freedom, the dwellings are not accessed directly from the street. 'Indentations' in the block give access to a sort of second surface level situated on the roof of the shops. The dwellings are accessed from here via two stairwells and short galleries. The columns framing the shops make it possible for shopkeepers to choose the material, form and colour of their shop fronts and advertisements without disturbing the unity of the design. As an interlude in the long street façade, 16 market-sector dwellings have been built in the middle, the 'fourth' block. It differs from the other blocks in that its façade is entirely of brick and so does not have the 'floating' character of the other blocks.

*Housing
Marnixstraat
[Jef Reintjens,
1997]*

'Städte bauen heisst: mit dem Hausmaterial Raum gestalten', said art historian A.E. Brinckmann in 1908. And the urban space shows us how true this still is.

The traditional urban space consists of streets and squares, and the street façades and the walls of squares define this space. It has often been said that as a result these façades have a dual character: they give architectural shape to a building and determine the appearance of a street or a square. Not surprisingly, this duality was unacceptable to the rationalistically minded Functionalists, some sixty years ago. The *rue corridor* had to go in order to make way for a radical form of zoning: freestanding residential buildings in open green space.

Already in the fifties and sixties, however, it became clear that the ideal of the functional city did not function in reality. Urban life is far more complex than the Functionalists had supposed and there was a growing realization that the traditional street channels this complexity far more successfully than the functional city's public space, which is scarcely, if at all, architecturally defined.

Partly because of pressure from local residents, it soon became common practice when renewing old residential districts to preserve the existing street patterns with their closed blocks. Amsterdam now has a quarter of a century of experience with this working method, and it is clear that the traditional duality of the urban frontage has made a triumphant comeback. It is interesting therefore to compare the results of recent years with the street façades of the prefunctional period.

This comparison shows that there has been an almost ironical reversal. The then chairman of the Congrès Internationaux d'Architecture Moderne (CIAM), C. van Eesteren, had to explain to Amsterdam's by and large unlettered architects that row housing is quite different from a block without ends, and the results of Van Eesteren's evening classes can still be seen in the prewar area of the district of Bos en Lommer. Today, it is the Building Inspectorate which has to explain to dogmatic Functionalist architects that inserting new buildings in an existing block is quite different from designing a shorter or longer section of row housing. It is becoming increasingly clear why H.P. Berlage characterized (in 1893) his assembled colleagues as 'an art proletariat'.

Experience has shown that the renovation of existing housing complexes always produces a better result than demolition followed by new development. Partly because of the revival of interest in the architecture of the Amsterdam School, many blocks in residential districts of the period 1920-40 have been so carefully renovated that we can almost speak of restoration. This is a recognition of the fact that these blocks are not isolated monuments but form part of an urbanistic unity.

Evidence to bear this out can be found in the city's nineteenth-century districts. Here, there is little appreciation of the architecture, so that demolition is an easy option. The old building lines are usually respected in the new development, but the typology of the original buildings is invariably replaced by an entirely different typology. The result is a hybrid monster of nineteenth-century street profiles and pseudo-functional architecture which is ludicrously out of place.

Amsterdam's nineteenth-century street façades are characterized by the coercive rhythm of the doors (two front doors every six metres) and by the powerful horizontal lines of the windows in the three storeys above. The façades are terminated by a bold, white cornice line above which is a row of attic windows and hoisting beams. In cases where only a few structures have been demolished and replaced by new buildings, the results are particularly disastrous. Because the new building is accessed in a different way, and also because of the wide variety of window-frames, the new sections of street frontage are often completely out of harmony with the surrounding buildings.

These nineteenth-century streets never had any particular aesthetic merit, but this is what makes them so special. Their austerity and restraint show up the pretentious new buildings which all too often mar the streetscape (see, for example, Quellijnstraat in De Pijp, pp. 60-61, and Marnixstraat in De Jordaan). The unity of the façades is easily destroyed and the wealth of architectural devices which characterizes much new development does not result in a new unity, but in a chaos which is worse than the original austerity.

Clearly, making a section of a nineteenth-century street façade autonomous through demolition and replacement by new buildings is the wrong choice, both urbanistically and architecturally. Only when a complete street frontage is replaced by a new architectural unity can something of urbanistic significance come into being. A good example of this can be seen in Eerste van Swindenstraat (see pp. 66-67).

The architecture here calls to mind the blocks by Erwin Gutkind in Berlin of the twenties, and thus deserves praise. However, one is also immediately reminded of, for example, Jan Evertsenstraat in Amsterdam-West, designed in 1925 by J.F. Staal, which is clearly superior. Staal, so it seems, was more sure of himself, and therefore dared to opt for an extreme simplicity and – honesty compels me to admit it – was able to apply detailing which lends the austere street façade a wonderful splendour. Contemporary architecture lacks such craftsmanship.

The reverse of what we see in Eerste van Swindenstraat can be seen in small-scale renewal projects where one or two, at most three, narrow plots are rebuilt. The small scale means that the original typology is retained, and when the architect is also prepared to take the surrounding buildings into account in his choice of materials the result is a form of urban renewal which is almost traditional. Indeed the canal-side façades have for centuries been undergoing this process of renewal.

The architectural idiom does not have to be historicizing. Indeed, it is an interesting fact that small-scale old building development can, within limits, incorporate small-scale modern development. The new buildings in Haarlemmerstraat and Haarlemmerdijk demonstrate that the street façades of very old inner-city streets can absorb changes while preserving their original character.

VINCENT VAN ROSSEM

Office and information centre New Deal, Van Eesterenlaan
(Heren 5 architecten, 1995)

In 1995 the development company New Deal held a competition for temporary office accommodation. The idea was for an eye-catching pavilion which could accommodate the estate agents' office for the dwellings being realized on Borneo/Sporenburg, two peninsulas in the Oostelijk Havengebied (Eastern Docklands). The brief required an identifiable image, because the office was to be situated in an area where an entire residential district is under construction, and which lacks urban spaces such as squares and streets.

Heren 5 won the competition with a design for a structure which attracts the attention of the visitor by a light-column. The pavilion is composed of ready-made building units, linked together to house all the offices and other spaces. Rough planks function as the entrance, sun-blinds for the building units and as a roof for the presentation, conference and film rooms. The entrance and the exhibition space are situated on the first floor. When the district is finished, the office will be redundant and will be demolished. The planks can be reused and the building units (on which there is a deposit) returned to the manufacturer.

Floor plans dwellings

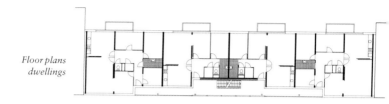

20 dwellings, Vrolikstraat (Duinker, Van der Torre, 1994)
The commission which Duinker, Van der Torre received for Vrolik-straat was for the infilling of a 44-metre gap. The streetscape is determined by dark, nineteenth-century façades and a relatively narrow profile. The aim was to enliven this image by constructing a façade with a strong horizontal character and a large glazed wall to contrast with the surroundings. The façade is divided into a ground floor, middle section and upper storey. The ground floor is composed of ashlar and wooden window-frames. The materials used above are pale brick, wood and aluminium. The upper storey is set back and has a canopy at gutter level which emphasizes the distinction between middle section and upper storey. The dwellings themselves are set back from the building line. This creates a zone for access by way of short galleries which can be reached via the stairwell behind the glass wall. On the ground floor are two dwellings for the disabled. The five dwellings on the top floor have been designed for a commune. An important point of departure was optimal flexibility in the dwellings, which is why there are sliding walls between the rooms.

Façade

24 dwellings, Vrolikstraat (Steigenga Smit architekten, 1996)
In 1990 a plan was launched for the refurbishment of a housing block at the beginning of Vrolikstraat in Amsterdam-Oost. This plan was abandoned, however, when it became clear that it would be too costly. As part of a planning study, Steigenga Smit then drew up a scheme for a new building. Points of departure were an economic building plan and optimal orientation to the sun. The structure has a simple frame with, in the rhythm of the porch access, three recesses. These lead to the stairwells on the rear elevation. The ground floor contains six dwellings with a higher (work) space on the street, behind which, at a lower level, is a kitchen. The second and third storeys contain *casco* dwellings with only the most basic provisions (a core housing the kitchen and sanitary facilities). The fourth and fifth storeys contain maisonettes.

The design fits in with the Vrolikstraat façade, which is characterized by the rhythm of the porch access and the combination of living and working on the ground floor. The façade on the street side is clad with brick, the rear elevation is of wood. The appearance of this rear wall is determined by the glass panels of the stairwells and the balconies which are aligned with the stairs.

Cross-section
and
floor plan
dwellings

De Tagrijn

*Vespucci-
straat*

➤

82 dwellings and commercial premises, Vespuccistraat,

Bartholomeus Diazstraat (Meyer & Van Schooten, 1994 and 1995)
Vespuccistraat is situated in the Mercatorplein district, a neighbourhood characterized by the architecture of the Amsterdam School. Some of the characteristics of this architecture, such as towers and the use of brick, have been incorporated in the new development. The project consists of three blocks. On Vespuccistraat are two virtually symmetrical blocks containing 58 dwellings and 5 commercial premises. Because a market is held in this street, the block has been raised half a storey so that occupants on the ground floor can look out over the market stalls. The ground floor in the corner 'towers' contain the commercial spaces. The façade at the front comprises an aluminium grid in a brick frame. Within this grid are the balconies, which are staggered per storey. The stairwells are situated next to the 'towers' in the side streets and are linked to continuous galleries via which the dwellings are accessed.

The third block, De Tagrijn, is situated in Bartholomeus Diazstraat. This block contains 24 dwellings behind a glazed screen. This screen masks the individuality of the dwellings.

'Skydome', 100 dwellings, KNSM-*laan* (Wiel Arets, 1995)

The point of departure for the sixty-metre high residential tower on KNSM-eiland was that it had to be a slender tower and it had to conform to the building lines in Jo Coenen's urban design plan for the area. The building, called Skydome, with the nickname the Zwarte Weduwe (black widow), contains 100 owner-occupied apartments on 22 floors. The façade is composed of concrete elements with a dark grey relief which looks like natural stone. Deep joints in the façade suggest that the building consists of four sections. The tower's height is accentuated by its slenderness, but is neutralized by the strong horizontal lines of the loggias.

The standard storey contains five apartments, three of which are orientated to the south, and two to the north. The latter command a view over the IJ. All dwellings have a balcony. The socle of the building contains an underground car park, above which is a semi-public pedestrian deck with the entrances to the lifts.

*Emerald
Empire*
Jo Coenen,
[1995]

Amsterdam is an angular city. True, the old city is famous for its seemingly circular seventeenth-century plan, but if we look carefully we see that the so-called 'concentric' canals are not curved at all. They consist, like the threads in a spider's web, of straight stretches which are slightly at an angle to each other.

Other parts of Amsterdam are also noticeably straight. The layout of the old working-class district De Jordaan follows the pattern of the old drainage channels, and the rectangular grid of the old polders was retained in the planning of the nineteenth-century city expansions. Berlage's famous design for Plan Zuid has very few curves, and Amsterdam's Algemeen Uitbreidingsplan (General Extension Plan) by C. van Eesteren is, as might be expected of an ex-member of De Stijl, a tribute to orthogonal planning.

The angularity of Amsterdam's street layout has never been counterbalanced by its buildings. Amsterdam has few old round buildings and the ones that are round are not conspicuously so. For example, the Ronde Lutherse Kerk (Adriaan Dortsman, 1671) on Singel is surrounded by angular houses which mask its shape.

It is a cliché, but nevertheless irresistibly tempting, to say that the lack of curves in Amsterdam is due to Calvinism. Round is voluptuous, baroque, Roman Catholic, and not dour Protestant. And, whether Catholic or not, round is certainly theatrical. Ancient Roman theatres were semicircular, Greek theatres were slightly more circular. An amphitheatre such as the Colosseum in Rome is oval. And when a round building was not a theatre, it was a tomb, temple, church, baptistery, villa or a folly. Buildings, in short, with a special function, to which the circular form (it catches the eye and creates space) was admirably suited. Mycenaean rulers were buried in domed tombs, Roman emperors in circular mausoleums. Perhaps the most famous circular building is the Pantheon (the Roman temple of all the gods), which was to be the model for endless variations on the theme, from Palladio's Villa Rotonda near Vicenza to Soufflot's Panthéon in Paris.

Amsterdam, capital city of a country where sobriety is considered almost a national virtue, has evidently never had a need for *grandeur*. Well into the last century, Jacob van Campen's town hall (1648) on the Dam was the largest building in Amsterdam. It is extremely angular. Amsterdam's aversion to round buildings was so great that the city does not even have a panopticon – the customary prison design in the nineteenth century, with the state as the all-seeing eye.

The canals are lined with individual houses built by merchants who were hardly ever given the opportunity to break with the national custom of not displaying one's wealth. This was because the land along the canals was granted, by order of the city government, in narrow and deep plots, which meant that there was no room for circular buildings.

Against this background it is all the more remarkable that in recent years many circular buildings have been built in Amsterdam. It must have been the Stadhuis/Muziektheater, the curious town hall/opera house combination completed in 1986/87, which effected the circular building's breakthrough in Amsterdam. The architects, Cees Dam and Wilhelm Holzbauer, gave that part of the structure which contains the theatre foyer an expressive roundness. True, the façade, like the canals, is composed of straight sections, but its image was so prominent in all discussions from the moment the design was presented (1979) that it has rid Amsterdam of its historical fear of curves.

Since then a whole series of circular buildings has been realized. In 1990, a round, glass tower by Abma+Dirks+Partners was erected in one of the courtyards of the Nederlandsche Bank, an extremely angular building built in 1968 by M.F. Duintjer. Unfortunately, this round tower is, to paraphrase Prince Charles, a monstrous carbuncle on the face of a building which is not even that well loved. Far more successful are the semicircular refectory by the same architectural office (1988) and the Amsterdam University's oval information centre (Theo Bosch, 1994) in the grounds of the former Binnengasthuis, both of which are a fitting, joyous answer to the brick austerity of the old hospital pavilions.

In 1992 the headquarters of Wagons Lits, designed by Benthem Crouwel, was realized next to Centraal Station. For years this had been a desolate site where tramps died, unnoticed. The tower with two round sides and tropical sun screens, together with the adjacent hotel, put an end to this. Close by, on the other side of the railway line but still in old Amsterdam, is the Dutch rail company's traffic control centre, built in 1994 to a design by Rob Steenhuis (see pp. 48-49). A dominant feature of this structure is the large circular control room.

New circular buildings have been realized not only in the old city centre, but also in Amsterdam's new districts. In 1993, on a site on the edge of the city, in Amsterdam-Noord, Liesbeth van de Pol built the so-called 'trommelwoningen', cylinder-shaped structures with small inner courts. Also in Amsterdam-Noord, in 1996 Marlies Rohmer realized old people's dwellings in the form of Frank Lloyd Wright's Guggenheim Museum. In Nieuw Sloten, in 1995 a pair of oval towers was built, to a design by Atelier Pro, as accents in the new residential district. The apotheosis of the new circular Amsterdam is the colossal circular housing block which since 1996 has formed the dramatic termination of the long and narrow KNSM-eiland. It is surely no coincidence that this building was designed by Jo Coenen, who hails from Limburg in the Catholic south of the country.

More circular buildings have been built in Amsterdam in the last ten years than in all preceding centuries. And if, as many believe, architecture is a reflection of society, then this must signify something. If circular buildings are connected with theatricality, then one could conclude that Amsterdam has conquered its fear of the grand statement, and is no longer dominated by Calvinism or by Van Eesteren's Nieuwe Bouwen – the secularized, twentieth-century version of orthodox Protestantism in architecture. In its capital city Amsterdam, the country celebrates the fact that it has lost its faith by erecting circular buildings.

BERNARD HULSMAN

'De Branding', dwellings, shops, offices and underground car park,
Buikslotermeerplein (De Architectengroep – project architect:
Gert-Jan Hendriks, 1995)

The complex 'De Branding' is situated on the east side of Buikslotermeerplein in Amsterdam-Noord and forms part of the shopping centre
'Boven 't IJ'. The design was an entry for a competition, held by the city
council, aimed at finding a solution for housing on the edge of the shopping centre. The scheme consists of three parts, each of which is accessed
from Buikslotermeerplein.

A 19-storey tower, which functions as a landmark, contains 86
dwellings. The dwellings have an extravert character thanks to the
storey-high aluminium front which encloses the sun lounge and the
living-room. Immediately adjacent to the tower is the low-rise, which
consists of two parts. The ground floor of the low-rise contains shops,
cafés and restaurants, and offices. Above are 17 dwellings and offices on
two floors. The roof accentuates the difference between the offices and
the dwellings. The roof of the dwellings slopes down to the terrace
above the shops and the square. The roof of the offices is a mirror image
of this. The 175 parking spaces have been realized underground.

Mosque, dwellings and shops, Insulindeweg, Celebesstraat, Tomin), straat (Duinker, Van der Torre, 1993 and 1995)

The brief for this project specified a block which would function as a landmark for Indische Buurt and which would have a similar aura to that of the demolished block (built in 1920 by H.T. Wijdeveld) it was to replace. The project was realized in two phases. The first phase involved the construction of 48 dwellings and 4 shops. This housing block consists of two parts: a raised end on Insulindeweg and a smaller volume on Toministraat. At the corner with Celebesstraat is a wedge-shaped stairwell via which the dwellings are accessed. In the second phase, a mosque (on the ground floor) and 21 dwellings were added. The large sanctuary has a surface area of 450 square metres and is 5 metres high. The entrance to the mosque, situated at the front of the building, is a broad, elongated space which can be added to the sanctuary space. Situated on the first floor are the women's sanctuary and a number of classrooms. The design for the mosque was made in consultation with the Moroccan community. The dwellings above the mosque, all for the elderly, are accessed via a lift and short galleries at the rear of the building. These galleries are linked to the stairwell built in the first phase.

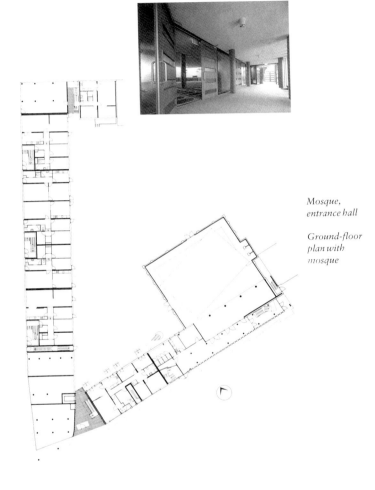

*Mosque,
entrance hall*

*Ground-floor
plan with
mosque*

Corridor

Children's day care centre JoJo, Wiltzanghlaan

(Architektengroep 69 Groenhout, 1994)

The programme for this site comprised a children's day care centre for three baby groups, three toddler groups and two after-school groups; in total over 100 children. Because of the site's limited surface area, the building has two storeys. For various reasons the floor plan is based on a stepped, diagonal composition. This form improves the connection with the buildings on the east side of the site. The roof overhang follows the building line and on the south side this creates a covered play area. There are long sight-lines from all group rooms. Because of the stepped composition, the corridor is divided into small play areas next to each classroom which are more or less enclosed.

For functional reasons the central facilities, such as the kitchen and office on the ground floor, are situated around the central play area. Here too are the spaces for the baby groups, each of which comprises a playroom and a bedroom and has direct access to the covered play area. The toddler groups and the after-school groups are situated on the first floor and have a play area on the north side of the building.

South and east façades

First- and ground-floor plan

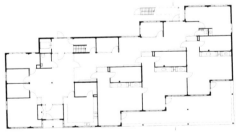

North and west façades

Dwellings, shops and car park, Beethovenstraat, Gerrit van der Veenstraat (Architektenburo Hans Bosch, 1996)

A unique site in H.P. Berlage's Plan Zuid, in one of the most important shopping streets, was occupied up until 1994 by a building with a garage and shops. This single-storey building was demolished to make way for a six-storey block. The programme for this complex comprised shops, a multi-storey car park and dwellings, with various care facilities, for the elderly. The dwellings are contained in a U-shaped block above shops in the street. Situated on the first floor, in the curve of the U, is a garden with a pond. Adjacent to this are the offices of a number of care agencies and a restaurant for residents and other elderly people in the neighbourhood. At the request of residents, the galleries have been screened off from the outside with glass walls and the colour scheme is warm. The two- and three-roomed flats have a built-in conservatory. Some of them also have a small balcony.

The ground floor in Beethovenstraat contains six shops. Behind (with the entrance in a side street) is a large supermarket. To facilitate deliveries to the supermarket an internal street has been designed with parking space for two trailers.

Roof garden

Cross-section

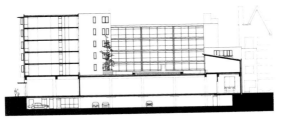

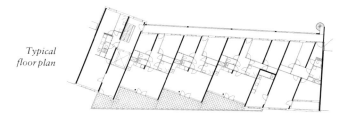

*Typical
floor plan*

29 dwellings, Victorieplein (Dobbelaar De Kovel De Vroom
   Architekten, 1994)

Victorieplein is situated at the intersection of three monumental axes in
Berlage's Plan Zuid and is determined by two large, closed building
blocks and a residential tower ('De Wolkenkrabber' built in 1928 to a
design by J.F. Staal). Dobbelaar De Kovel De Vroom took as the point of
departure for their design (the result of a limited competition) the architectural themes 'wall' and 'corner turn', which also determined the original building here. The division into ground floor, intermediate storey
and upper storeys, the arrangement of horizontal and vertical façade
openings, the oriel-like recess, the continuous canopy and the accentuation of the corner are all features which characterized the original architecture. The dwellings are accessed via galleries along the rear elevation.
These galleries are linked to a lift in the entrance hall, which is situated at
the corner. The apartments are all oriented to the square to the south
and negate, as it were, the corner turn. The dwellings on the ground
floor have a porch and are slightly raised on the street side to increase
residents' privacy. On the garden side this results in an extra high living-
room.

Housing Javastraat [Hans Wagner, 1995]

There was a time when building was an ordinary everyday activity. When Adam was expelled from Paradise he had to build himself a hut in order to find protection from unpredictable nature. And so the first dwelling programme was born, without it ever having been expressed in words. Shelter was the first step on the long road towards perfection.

Adam's hut shows that in the past primitive programmes have resulted in a primitive and primary architecture. But history also shows, for example, that the (Amsterdam) town house passed through various stages of programmatic and spatial complexity in its development. These two aspects are not always in the right proportion. Programmatic simplicity can go together with spatial refinement and complexity. But the reverse, namely the combination of programmatic ambiguity and spatial and constructional simplicity, also occurs.

It is therefore questionable whether an unambiguous relationship can be constructed between, on the one hand, programme, regulations and use and, on the other, architectural quality. The question is whether the perfect building presupposes a perfect programme. And does the perfect programme automatically result in perfect architecture?

Countless forms of public and private law, statutes and regulations laid down by central government, provincial and municipal authorities regulate building and architectural production. In Europe and world-wide, an increasing number of agreements are being signed in order to internationalize policy decisions. In the Netherlands, the statutory framework is in theory aimed at deregulation, but in building practice it is experienced as an inflexible and restrictive complex of rules. This is primarily due to the raft of norms and directives.

Even more complicated than laws and legislation, however, are the programmes derived from practice. New ideas and developments in the construction industry improve product quality, productivity and working conditions, and this in turn results in an ongoing process of observation, research and the dissemination of findings, in which companies play a leading role. Increasingly, attention is being focused on housing processes, building management and design processes. The aim is an effective control over the integral building process in order to achieve favourable price-quality ratios and business results. Fundamental research is linked to frameworks for market-orientated projects.

Thus, a far-reaching influence is being exerted on building, which increasingly results in a certain 'overvaluation' of programmatic process and management aspects in the design, preparation and realization of space and architecture. Slowly but surely, the programmatic conditions of techniques and processes seem to be winning out and sometimes the programme threatens to overrun the architectural concept. The monofunctional residential areas are striking examples of this, but shopping and leisure centres, too, frequently demonstrate a programmatic overdose, which can be fatal for the weak constitution of the historic city centres in which they are often situated.

Certainly in the case of the Netherlands, it can be said that public housing was, and is, under political and bureaucratic control, both as regards financing and subsidizing and as regards the programme and the standardization of quality. Even now, despite the fact that increasingly housing production is in the hands of market-orientated and commercial bodies, the various layers of government still play a dominant role. This, among other things, in order to preclude the preponderance of one income group.

At the same time, government still exercises control over countless quality components of housing. The large municipalities in particular have their own guidelines (based on previous directives for the allocation of government funds) for public housing quality. In Amsterdam, for instance, great emphasis is placed on harmonizing specific groups, types of dwelling and location. Although flexibility is considered important, detailed directions are given regarding matters such as the layout of dwellings, materials, constructions and installations, sound proofing and building methods designed for durability. The city districts and clients apply these directives in contracts and projects in all financial categories. The municipal armamentarium in the form of various sur-charges is also geared to achieving this administratively and politically determined level of quality. A noteworthy fact in this respect is that with special housing programmes considerable influence is exerted on the dwelling differentiation for each project – an outstanding example of programmatic control.

Many technical and programmatic regulations can be characterized as bureaucratic and technocratic achievements (in a positive sense) aimed at improving safety, health and utility for a broad group of people. One of the problems which can arise is that it is sometimes diffi-cult to integrate, in an institutional way, the functions living and work-ing in a spatial coherence, while this coherence is the historical basis of, for example, the spatial richness of the city and the town house.

In a densely populated country like the Netherlands, the city is an important context for every building task. Every proposal is tested against its relationship with its surroundings, and the city is thus an important programmatic condition which has not always been ad-equately defined in planning terms. Nevertheless, this is a real under-pinning for the quality of building and architecture. The city as morpho-logical programme is indispensable as part of the integral programme for the built architecture. Even if there was a perfect architectural pro-gramme, only perfect urbanism would make the perfect building or the perfect architecture possible.

It is thus a question of clearly defining both the urbanistic conditions and the programmatic points of departure. And this is imperative now that the specialism is becoming seriously fragmented. There is no rem-edy against the staggering and ever-increasing number of international norms. Even the most perfect client is handicapped by this state of affairs, the most perfect programme is affected by it, perfection will never result from it.

MARINUS OOSTENBRINK

North façade

*Corridor
first floor* ➤

*Laboratory and lecture rooms, Biology Faculty, University of
Amsterdam, Anna's Hoeve* (Benthem Crouwel Architekten, 1995)
The main structure of the laboratory for molecular cytology is simple.
The building is raised, so that traffic on the surface level is not impeded
and the entrances are visible on all sides. It is situated between two existing buildings and is linked to them via elevated walkways. This solution
gives rise to one long internal circulation system with which users can
reach all parts of the biology complex. It also increases the flexibility of
the buildings. The corridor on the first floor functions as access corridor
for the building and is also a meeting space. It therefore plays a central
role in the complex and this has been expressed in the detailing. For
example, along the walls on either side illuminated glass strips have been
incorporated in the floor and the ceiling. The corridor is slightly off-
centre, as a result of which the rooms are not all the same size. On one
side are the offices without climate control, on the other side are the
climate-controlled laboratory and lecture rooms. The technical infrastructure is housed in a hollow wall on the south side. All installations
are situated on the top floor of the building in a block which seems to
hover above the building.

West façade

61 apartments for the elderly, offices, shops and car park, Osdorp-plein, Tussenmeer (OD 205 architectuur – project architect: Peter Defesche, 1996)

The housing block by OD 205 forms part of the large-scale refurbishment and extension scheme for the Osdorpplein shopping centre in Amsterdam-West. The building is situated on a corner and forms the link between Osdorpplein shopping centre and the residential and shopping street Tussenmeer. The points of departure for the building were the connection between the two shopping areas and the avoidance of 'rear sides'. The result is a differentiated complex.

A two-storey building with car park and shops extends Tussenmeer's shop frontage around the corner to Osdorpplein. Above this, parallel with the square, is an elongated apartment building, another eight storeys high. This is in keeping with the character of the large housing blocks in the surrounding neighbourhoods. Directly above the shops is a storey with storage spaces which forms an additional buffer between the shops and the apartments. The apartments are oriented west-east and are accessed via galleries. At the head end of the building are larger apartments which are oriented to the south.

*Façade
Osdorpplein*

*Floor plan
dwellings*

'Gulden Kruis', housing estate, Bijlmerdreef, Groesbeekdreef
(Architektenburo L. Lafour & R. Wijk, 1996)

This project for 213 dwellings marked the start of the large-scale regeneration of the Bijlmermeer. The regeneration is aimed at creating a more attractive and safer living environment, to be achieved by building mainly ground-accessed dwellings, together with measures in the field of the management and design of public space.

So-called 'up-down dwellings' have been built on the through routes Bijlmerdreef and Groesbeekdreef. These dwellings are two stacked maisonettes, both of which are accessed from the street. The zone two metres from the façade is for access and to bridge the differences in height. Behind these dwellings is a residential area with low-rise situated around the church De Nieuwe Stad (built in 1993 to a design by Lafour & Wijk). This low-rise consists of 15 blocks containing mostly single-family dwellings bordering on closed inner courts, which increases security. There is a great diversity of dwellings, but all are characterized by unevenly projecting roof surfaces which give rise to an upper light. The area is edged with wide strips of green space.

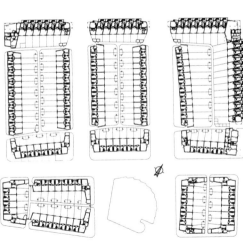

Main stand

'De Toekomst', Ajax youth training centre, stadium, Borchlandweg
(René van Zuuk architecten, 1996)

This project forms part of the new accommodation in Amsterdam-Zuidoost for the Amsterdam football club Ajax. The first team is accommodated in Amsterdam Arena and a new building has been constructed close by for youth training and the reserve team. Van Zuuk received the commission to design a sports and administrative complex covering 4,000 square metres, including the complete interior, two stands, dugouts, backstops and a building for the sale of tickets.

The main building consists of six segments with shed roofs which slot into each other. As a result, a chink of light falls in the spaces below. On the ground floor are the changing rooms, the physiotherapy rooms and the gymnasium. The first floor houses offices and a canteen.

The shape of the shed roofs is repeated in the curved form of the main stand with its 1,250 seats. The main stand's canopy is supported by a thick arcuate steel tube which hangs from the front of the roof on steel cables. This tube is connected to two masts, so that there is an uninterrupted view of the pitch. The curved structure echoes Arena's similar structure – Ajax youth teams' ultimate goal.

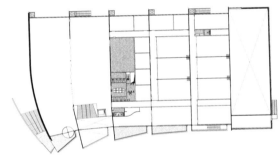

Main building, entrance and first-floor plan

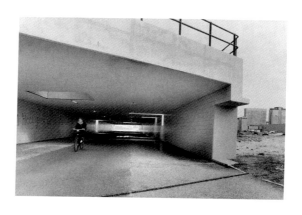

Cycle and pedestrian tunnels, Holterbergweg and surroundings
(Quist Wintermans Architekten, 1996)

The new Arena stadium occupies a prominent place in a large area in Amsterdam-Zuidoost which is being developed and which is also to have mega-stores, a mega-cinema and theatres. As part of the infrastructure near the stadium, Quist Wintermans has designed a number of viaducts, a pedestrian tunnel and a cycle/pedestrian tunnel. A key point of departure in the design was public safety, which is an extremely important aspect of this type of structure – especially in an area where there is no housing. The cycle/pedestrian tunnel on Burgemeester Stramanweg exemplifies the designers' principles. This concrete tunnel is approximately 120 metres long. It is characterized by large areas of striking colours and 'gaps' in the walls and ceilings. These gaps mean that the user has contact with the outside, reducing the feeling of being enclosed.

Bridge to
KNSM- *and*
Java-eiland
[Hans van
Heeswijk,
1996]

This essay is about bridges, tunnels and other traffic structures in and around the city. Flyovers and underpasses, noise barriers, in short: the objects which, rather confusingly, are called structural artworks.

Bridges and tunnels. There is no greater contrast. They are each other's opposites. The bridge over something – in the Netherlands usually over water – open, light, commanding a view. The tunnel, beneath or through something – closed, dark, hidden. Like positive and negative, black and white, this is how they relate to each other. Nevertheless they fulfil the same function: they provide a connection, making passage possible. The bridge forms part of the architectural fabric of the city, the tunnel does not. The bridge can be aesthetically appreciated for its purely constructional qualities, but also as an object embellished with sculptures. The engineer's bridge is slender and functional, the art bridge is expressive and has a specific character.

Recent examples of bridges in Amsterdam include the bridge for cyclists and pedestrians near Centraal Station, designed by Benthem Crouwel (1992) and the bridge in the Verbindingsdam to K N S M-eiland by Hans van Heeswijk. Both have been carefully designed and detailed, but this does not as yet point to a new trend. I need only quote examples such as the Berlagebrug over the Amstel, or a bridge in the city centre by Piet Kramer embellished with phantasmagoric creatures, to show that there is nothing new under the sun. The bridge keeps up with fashion and is necessarily a product of its time. And it will always be so, whether the designer is an engineer, an artist or an architect.

Although I love and enjoy bridges, tunnels have a greater appeal for me. Tunnels are indeterminate dark places which afford a glimpse of the city's belly. Here, you can see undersides – beams and other constructions. Here, a junkie shoots up, a tramp lies beneath a cardboard box, flashers lie in wait for schoolgirls and housewives. Small boys set off bangers, and bored adolescents empty aerosol cans of paint. Frayed edges, no man's land, nowhere is the anonymity of the city so perceptible as here.

I remember that as a child I used to go and sit beneath the railway bridge at certain times, on the embankment which was no longer an embankment but an underground space. This place had a certain isolation and you felt good there alone. I closed my eyes and waited. I waited for a faint rumble in the distance which gradually grew louder until a thunderous symphony exploded above my head, leaving my body trembling, full of adrenaline. A child's kick? Flirting with danger? Increasing the danger, putting myself to the test – secret danger? Perhaps these are ingredients for a therapy for stressed-out modern man. Imagination, such places appeal to one's imagination, like the dark forest where you imagine a monster lurking behind every tree. The magic of fear.

Today, tunnels are being systematically divested of these characteristics in order to make them safe and pleasant. They are embellished with works of art and neutralized with lights. No longer autonomous spatial objects, they are places, and increasingly architects are engaged to design these utilitarian objects. Take, for example, the tunnels and viaducts near Arena Stadium, designed by Quist Wintermans (see pp. 108-9). More and more local authorities launch competitions in which architects, landscape architects or artists take part. Recently, this was the case for the noise barriers along the A 10 in Amsterdam-Noord and for a bridge to Java-eiland.

So it seems that something has changed after all. It also seems as if there is now an awareness that a road is an aesthetic part of the landscape, and that passageways can be beautiful and should be carefully designed – in the same way in which in recent years more and more squares have been designed as part of the public space. This is an aesthetic awareness which follows naturally from the embellishment of public space with sculptures; only in this case art and object are one. But, moreover, there is also the discovery of the psychological dimension.

The Dutch architecture magazine *Archis* (1989-9) describes the noise barriers along the A 10 as a 'futuristic bobsleigh run, which will give the motorist the thrilling feeling that he will want to travel faster than light'. And: 'In order to enlarge the user's introvert environment and to prevent him becoming alienated from his surroundings, the barrier is criss-crossed with narrow, staggered horizontal slits, behind which the outside world appears in zootrope images.' What does this jargon mean?

I have always understood that the barriers are not there for the motorist to experience, but just to protect those who live next to the road. When architecture magazines and motorists notice the roadside, which previously had been dull and ugly, then something unusual is taking place. These barriers suddenly have a front and a rear side.

Since postmodernism, meaning and interpretation have been the focus of interest. In this light, structural artworks can be conceived as arresting urban signs which emphasize and determine the character of a district or a site. In so doing, however, the inner perception, the experience of the passer-by, the traveller is also designed and guided.

Structural works are in this respect disparate things: traffic object, element in the landscape, articulated site; but they are always connected with movement. And whatever the immediate reason for the increased interest on the part of local authorities, architects, artists and engineers in this aspect of urban planning, the underlying cause is the overorganized character of this small country, which is becoming increasingly cultivated, ordered and organized and where emptiness and indeterminacy are rapidly disappearing.

Sometimes I would like to put a stop to this tendency to aestheticize and control everything. I feel oppressed in a country where planning and design are taking over, where everything is so neat and tidy and planned; stifled by user-friendliness.

FREDERIKE HUYGEN

Rear façade

*Façade
Ookmeerweg*
➤

Residential care complex of 100 dwellings, Ookmeerweg
(MVRDV, 1996-97)

Ookmeerweg is situated in Amsterdam's Westelijke Tuinsteden (garden suburbs) which were built after the war to an urban design plan by C. van Eesteren (General Extension Plan, 1935). In the mid-nineties, a large-scale densification operation was launched here. As part of this operation, a commission was awarded for the construction of a box-shaped gallery flat with 100 apartments for people aged 55 and over. The brief specified that the principles of the garden suburb (for example, open green space) be retained. It became clear, however, that the proposed volume could accommodate only 87 dwellings. In order to accommodate the required 100 dwellings, the remaining 13 are housed in five small blocks suspended from the north wall of the slab by means of a steel construction. Four of the blocks have two storeys, the fifth has only one storey. The depth of the blocks equals that of the slab. The 'appendage dwellings', clad with red cedar, are oriented east-west. The apartments in the slab are oriented north-south. This has resulted in a south façade characterized by the balconies in different colours and sizes.

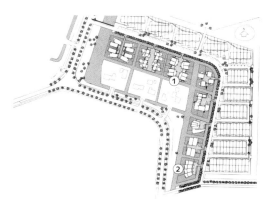

*Housing by
Oorthuys (1)
and Edhoffer
Van Exel (2)*

8 dwellings, Kortrijk, Nieuw Sloten (Fenna Oorthuys, 1995)
A series of islands has been developed as a link between the old village of
Sloten and the district of Nieuw Sloten. The client invited 24 women
architects to take part in a competition for the design of housing. The
number of dwellings required varied from four for the small islands to
eight for the larger islands. The commission was finally awarded to
seven architectural practices, one of which was Fenna Oorthuys.

Oorthuys' point of departure was that the island should have the
rural atmosphere of the village and her design is therefore characterized
by restraint. The eight dwellings (four semi-detached structures) are on
one side oriented to the water between the islands, and on the other side
to each other, around an oval exterior space. The island is rather small
for eight dwellings and so there is little privacy in the gardens. This is
compensated for by the roof terrace.

The floor plans of the adjoining dwellings are mirror-imaged.
Daylight enters the dwelling along the sloping roof via a glass front. The
core of the house is a void which provides light to all floors. Bordering
on this is the extra high living-room. A spiral staircase is a connecting
element through the void to the upper floors and the roof terrace.

4 dwellings, Kortrijk, Nieuw Sloten
(Edhoffer Van Exel architecten, 1995)

Like Fenna Oorthuys (see pp. 116-17), Edhoffer Van Exel was one of the seven architectural practices to be awarded a commission for development on an island on the edge of Nieuw Sloten.

The basic form is fan-shaped. The narrow side of the fan faces the entrance, the broad side faces the waterside garden. Because the dwellings are wider on this side, and because the rear walls are partly set back and the dwellings have been shifted slightly in relation to each other, there is maximum privacy. The dwellings have been arranged so as to minimize the fragmentation of the exterior space.

The four dwellings have the canalside house as archetype. Each dwelling has two entrances. One entrance leads directly to the space behind the carport, the other to the first floor via an external staircase within the structural walls. The result is flexibility with, for example, work space below and living above. A staircase in a small void against the rear wall connects the upper floor with the garden. The façades are executed in western red-cedar panels with a transparent finish.

Nieuw Sloten,
with housing by
Fenna Oorthuys (1),
Edhoffer Van Exel (2),
De Architectengroep (3)
and Sjoerd Soeters (4)

400 dwellings, Laan van Vlaanderen and surroundings

(De Architectengroep – project architect: Hans Ruijssenaars, 1995) This design for a district comprising 400 dwellings forms part of the plan to create a number of subareas, each with its own identity, in Nieuw Sloten. Ruijssenaars has designed a neighbourhood with a symmetrical layout. All street façades are three storeys high with closed corners. The long perimeter blocks and the closed corners emphasize the urban and framed character of the district. An important point of departure for the design was the relationship between the individual and the community. This is why the dwelling has been conceived as a component of the neighbourhood and not as an individual house. To emphasize this, in each dwelling the volume is concentrated on the street side. On the garden side – the private side – the dwelling is less high to maximize the entrance of sunlight in the gardens.

The green area in the heart of the district functions as the carrier of the plan. The parking spaces are situated in this central area. A continuous cycle route runs right through the area. It passes beneath a drumshaped building containing a commercial space and four dwellings.

151 dwellings and 12 water side dwellings, Blankenbergsestraat and surroundings (Sjoerd Soeters Architecten, 1995)

The low-rise dwellings by Sjoerd Soeters are situated on the edge of Nieuw Sloten, on a wedge-shaped site which forms the link between the rectangular subplans and the district's curved outer boundary. The aim was to combine the advantages of the traditional street with the advantages of 'open row housing' oriented to the sun. Soeters was able to fill most of the plan with two dwelling types. One type (with the sun on the street façade) has a kitchen/dining-room which is slightly raised on the street side with a narrow strip of terrace. The second type is oriented to the garden side with only a small kitchen on the street side.

The south façades are of white painted wood, the others are of brown-black and bright orange brick, except for those of the dwellings at the head ends. These dwellings form the boundary both of this plan and of Nieuw Sloten, and this is why they are decked out with eye-catching 'Zeeland caps' (named after the lace caps of the traditional Zeeland costume). On the ground floor, the floor plans follow the street façade, but the storeys above are oriented to the water. This is repeated in the six double dwellings on the water side.

Façade

17 dwellings, Monte Viso (Geurst & Schulze architekten, 1995)
A residential area comprising some 3,200 dwellings is being developed in a former market-gardening area in Osdorp. This expansion area, 'De Aker', is bounded on its southern edge by Haarlemmermeer's Ringvaart. Situated on the drainage channel which borders this is a strip of large luxury houses. Seventeen of these have been built to a design by Geurst & Schulze. These terrace houses are eight metres wide. An important point of departure in the design was optimal privacy and freedom of choice in the use of the various rooms. To this end, a difference in level has been created between the street and the drainage channel. The living-room is situated at a lower level, like a pavilion, on the water and is half the width of the house. By extending this part of the house to the water, the exterior space is screened off from the next-door house. The main volume is concentrated on the street side and is three storeys high. Situated on the street side is the sunken kitchen/dining-room, above which are the bedrooms. On the top storey is a roof terrace which commands a view over the dike. The façades consist of large areas of white concrete blocks interspersed with slabs of dark concrete brick.

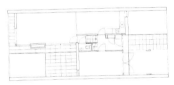

*Rear
elevation*

*Ground-floor
plan*

Cross-section

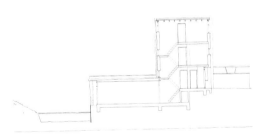

Office building [Van den Oever, Zaaijer, Roodbeen & Partners, 1995]

When reviewing the new architecture of a certain period, very often the emphasis is automatically and tacitly placed on new buildings. In some cases, however, the remodelling of an old building is a renewal with the allure and aura of a new building – to the extent that questions are raised regarding the differences between new-build and the remodelling of an existing structure, and the relevance of this for the way in which a city changes over time.

In Amsterdam in recent years there have been a number of cases where an existing building has been given a new appearance. Sometimes a real metamorphosis has taken place, usually because the building was outmoded as regards climate control and/or technical installations. Because the solution to the problem of insulation lies logically in the outer skin, the renewal process necessarily begins with the façade. But when a new façade image comes into being, this always means a new identity. Which is why of course the reverse also occurs, namely façades are replaced which technically do not (yet) need replacing.

The phenomenon of façade transformation is not new. The history of architecture provides numerous examples, in different periods and in different countries, of buildings whose façade was as it were a project in itself. In the Renaissance, many churches were given a façade years after the building had been inaugurated. Take, for example, the fifteenth-century Santa Maria del Fiore in Florence, which for a great many years had a bare and humble appearance due to lack of funds and indecision. It was only when these problems had been overcome that the church was given the polychrome marble façade we know today.

A historical example in Amsterdam of a façade transformation is the building on Oude Turfmarkt which now houses the Allard Pierson Museum. In 1841 the Dutch government provided two buildings on this site as accommodation for the Nederlandsche Bank. When the bank outgrew the building, several adjoining plots were acquired and the whole was combined in 1864 behind the wide neoclassicist front by W.A. Froger, which still exists today.

Whoever thinks that things are different nowadays is mistaken. On Weteringschans stands the steel frame of what used to be Winter department store (J. Duiker, 1934). This, however, has been radically altered and the present façade (Hans Bosch, 1982) is not in the least reminiscent of the lightness which characterizes Duiker's work. Likewise, few people know that the office tower on Weesperzijde, revamped in 1987 by Ben Loerakker, is the building Mart Stam built in 1963 for Mahuko. Another example of such a transformation is the pair of neoclassicist office buildings, by the architects Groenendaal & De Vries, which since 1995 has stood on Museumplein. It was formed by making the two parts of a modern office building (Ad. Polak, 1965) autonomous.

The phenomenon is particularly significant at the present moment because large-scale renewal processes, which will inevitably result in a new image, are taking place in the city. The postwar districts in particular are being renewed. A radical renewal was that by J. Franso & Partners in 1988 of the dwellings on Populierenweg in Amsterdam-Oost, built in 1952 by H.T. Zwiers. This was one of the first examples of industrial housing in the Netherlands in which the so-called Airey system was used. In the refurbishment, the prefabricated concrete façade panels characteristic of this system disappeared behind insulation and plaster layers. Such operations have also been carried out, or are in preparation, in the Westelijke Tuinsteden. A spectacular refurbishment is that of the block of flats 'Hoogoord' (Verheijen/Verkoren/de Haan, 1995). This building, designed by Kees Rijnboutt in 1968, was the first housing block to be completed in the Bijlmermeer (Amsterdam-Zuidoost). Partly because it occupies a key location – close to the shopping centre 'De Amsterdamse Poort' and the Bijlmer railway and metro station – and has therefore a more powerful aura than less favourably situated structures, it was also the first building to be refurbished as part of the urban regeneration of the Bijlmermeer. In the original building, the lower storeys contained storage spaces, bleak underpasses and a dreary inner street. Many people regarded the immediate vicinity as desolate and unsafe. For this reason, the first two storeys have been rebuilt and now contain dwellings which are accessed directly from the (new) street and which are situated around a new communal garden. Access to the upper storeys has also been improved. The result is quite remarkable. Blind walls have been replaced by transparent glass fronts, an anonymous exterior space is now an area for which all residents feel responsible.

Connected with such renewal projects is the phenomenon of the recycling of buildings, whereby a building is given a new purpose. In many cases, the new function is not visible in the cityscape. For example, a former pumping station now houses one of Amsterdam's trendiest restaurants ('Amsterdam'), but the exterior of the building reveals nothing of what goes on within. Sometimes, however, the image does change. When a large firm of solicitors moved into the building of the former Rijksverzekeringsbank on Apollolaan (D. Roosenburg, 1939), the circular base, which had previously housed archives, was turned into office space. Because of the need for parking space, the base was subsequently demolished and rebuilt (Liag Architekten, 1993), in a slightly altered form, with an underground car park. When the municipal department of sewers and water management needed new office space, the obvious choice was a new building on the existing sewage treatment site on Spaklerweg. A striking feature of the plan by Van den Oever, Zaaijer, Roodbeen & Partners (1995) were the three colossal concrete cylinders in which until recently sewage water had been treated, but which, it transpired, were also admirably suited for use as a conference room, canteen and fitness centre.

The inevitable and significant consequence of such transformations is that the city changes, as it were, insidiously. The viewer is presented with surprising questions, which chiefly have to do with the concepts of time and memory. It may at first seem that nothing much has changed, even in cases where ultimately, within a very short space of time, a radical transformation appears to have taken place. Afterwards, some find it difficult to remember what the building used to look like, while others find it difficult to get used to the new situation because they still have a clear picture of the building's original appearance. Images stored in the memory seem, as it were, to resist the adjustment which has taken place.

This is partly why it is such a complex phenomenon. The genesis of the projects inevitably leads to a multilayered structure, and it is up to the architect to deal with this. Furthermore, it is of course above all a question of whether this stratification is recognizable and is used in the design, or is negated. In all cases, the architect must take a stance with regard to what Robert Venturi has called the concept of the 'decorated shed'. An interesting example in Amsterdam is the architectural office of Sjoerd Soeters in Kerkstraat. In 1987 Soeters gave a Baptist chapel – built in the sixties, with a façade of ashlar and brick – a new aluminium screen. The form and the construction of the screen emphasize that this is an autonomous element which has been placed in front of the building, and which can easily be replaced at a future date if desired.

At the close of the twentieth century the architect must realize that the lifetime of a building is so limited that it is advisable when designing to bear in mind that the end result might be transformed in the not too distant future. And because a different architect is usually involved in a transformation, architects must resign themselves to the fact that what they regard as their spiritual property is not inviolable.

MAARTEN KLOOS

Hoogoord [Verheijen/ Verkoren/de Haan, 1995]

De Architectengroep bv (Gert-Jan Hendriks) · 'De Branding', dwellings, shops, offices, and car park, Buikslotermeerplein
Designed in: 1990;
with: Gini Corso, Francois le Roy, Bastiaan Vlierboom, Rob van der Vooren;
commissioned by: Delta Ontwikkelingsgroep vof, Dordrecht;
realized by: Bouwbedrijf Wessels Zeist, Zeist, 1995

De Architectengroep bv (Hans Ruijssenaars) · 400 dwellings, Laan van Vlaanderen and surroundings
Designed in: 1992;
with: Ed Schwier, Eric Heeremans, Peter Alberts, Jan Fraijman;
commissioned by: Woningbouwvereniging Ons Huis, Amsterdam, Woningbouwvereniging Amsterdam-Zuid, Amsterdam;
realized by: Bouwbedrijf M.J. de Nijs & Zn bv, Warmenhuizen, 1995

Architektengroep 69 Groenhout · Children's day care centre JoJo, Wiltzanghlaan
Designed in: 1992;
commissioned by: Stadsdeel Bos en Lommer, Amsterdam;
realized by: Intervam-Noordwest bv, Amsterdam, Homij, Amsterdam, 1994

De Architekten Cie. (Frits van Dongen) · 'My Side', 106 dwellings, Veemkade
Designed in: 1993;
with: A.J. Mout, L. Pires, R. Konijn;
commissioned by: Amstelland Vastgoed, Amsterdam;
realized by: Aannemingsbedrijf Teerenstra bv, Heiloo, 1995

Wiel Arets · 'Skydome', 100 dwellings, KNSM-laan
Designed in: 1990;
commissioned by: Bouwfonds Woningbouw, Hoevelaken, Wilma Bouw bv, Amsterdam;
realized by: Wilma Bouw bv, Amsterdam, 1995

Benthem Crouwel Architekten BNA (Mels Crouwel) · Laboratory and lecture rooms, Biology Faculty, University of Amsterdam, Anna's Hoeve
Designed in: 1994;
with: Joost Ruland;
commissioned by: Board of directors, University of Amsterdam;
realized by: Nubouw Nelis Uitgeest, 1995

Van Berkel & Bos Architectuurbureau bv, in collaboration with De Klerk Architecten · 'De Kolk', underground car park, office, hotel, 38 apartments, shops, cafés and restaurants, Nieuwezijds Kolk/Nieuwendijk
Designed in: 1990;
with: Harry Pappot, Jaap Punt, Martin Blokker;
commissioned by: ABN AMRO Projectontwikkeling bv, Amsterdam; Intell Hotel Exploitatiemaatschappij, Arnhem; Gemeente Amsterdam, afdeling parkeerbeheer;
realized by: Hollandsche Beton Maatschappij, Amsterdam; Aannemingsbedrijf H.J. Jurriëns bv, Utrecht, 1996

Architektenburo Hans Bosch · 63
dwellings for elderly people, shops, and
car park, Beethovenstraat/Gerrit van
der Veenstraat/Brahmsstraat
  Designed in: 1992-94;
  commissioned by:
  Woningbouwvereniging A C O B,
  Amsterdam, Stadsdeel Zuid,
  Amsterdam;
  realized by: Vink Bouw, Nieuwkoop
  bv, 1995-97

Claus en Kaan Architecten B N A bv ·
10 dwellings and commercial space,
Haarlemmerstraat/Binnenwieringer-
straat
  Designed in: 1990;
  with: Floor Arons, Roland Rens,
  Michiel van Pelt;
  commissioned by: Stichting Lieven
  de Key, Amsterdam;
  realized by: Grootel's
  Bouwmaatschappij bv, Maarssen,
  1995

Dobbelaar de Kovel de Vroom
Architekten bv · 29 dwellings,
Victorieplein
  Designed in: 1990-92;
  with: Thijs de Haan, Isaac Batenburg;
  commissioned by: Stichting
  Woningbedrijf Amsterdam,
  vestiging Amstel;
  realized by: E B A Amsterdam, 1994

Duinker, van der Torre, samenwer-
kende architecten (Machiel van der
Torre) · 20 dwellings, Vrolikstraat
  Designed in: 1991;
  with: Niels de Jong;
  commissioned by: Woningbouw-
  bedrijf Amsterdam;
  realized by: Bouw-aannemingsbedrijf
  Teerenstra bv, Heiloo, 1995

Duinker, Van der Torre, samenwer-
kende architecten (Margreet Duinker) ·
Mosque, dwellings and shops,
Celebesstraat/Insulindeweg
  Designed in: 1991/1993;
  with: John Buijs, Hens Burger, Cock
  Peterse, Liesbeth Wesseling;
  commissioned by: Stichting
  Woningbedrijf Amsterdam,
  Stadsdeel Zeebrug, Amsterdam;
  realized by: Intervam-Noordwest bv,
  Amsterdam, 1993, Florie en
  Van den Heuvel bv, Nieuwegein,
  1995

ir. Bart Duvekot – architect B N A ·
36 dwellings and 1 commercial premise,
Dapperstraat/Wijttenbachstraat
  Designed in: 1994;
  commissioned by: Woningbedrijf
  Centrum-Oost, Amsterdam;
  realized by: Bouwbedrijf V I O S b.v.,
  Utrecht, 1995

Edhoffer Van Exel architecten (Lisl
Edhoffer, Irene van Exel) · 4 dwellings,
Kortrijk, Nieuw Sloten
  Designed in: 1993-94;
  commissioned by: Wilma
  Vastgoed bv, Nieuwegein;
  realized by: Wilma Bouw,
  Amsterdam, 1995

Geurst & Schulze architekten bv
(Jeroen Geurst) · 17 dwellings, Monte
Viso
  Designed in: 1993;
  with: Robin van de Ven, Theo van
  de Beek;
  commissioned by: Smit's
  Bouwbedrijf, Beverwijk;
  realized by: Smit's Bouwbedrijf,
  Beverwijk, 1995

Hans van Heeswijk architect B N A bv ·
53 dwellings, Linnaeusstraat/
Commelinstraat/Dapperstraat/
Von Zesenstraat
  Designed in: 1993;
  with: P. Seuntjes;
  commissioned by: Woningstichting
  Lieven de Key, Amsterdam;
  realized by: Grootel Noord/West,
  Amsterdam, 1995

Heren 5 architecten · Office and infor-
mation centre New Deal bv, C. van
Eesterenlaan/Borneolaan
  Designed in: 1995;
  commissioned by:
  Ontwikkelingsmaatschappij New
  Deal bv;
  realized by: Intervam-Noordwest bv,
  Almere, 1995

Architektenburo L. Lafour en R. Wijk
bv · 213 dwellings and 2 commercial
permises, 'Gulden Kruis',
Bijlmerdreef/Groesbeekdreef
  Designed in: 1994;
  with: Stephen Reid, Trees Konijn,
  Niels Dönszelmann;
  commissioned by: Delta roA,
  Amsterdam;
  realized by: Bot Bouw,
  Heerhugowaard, 1995-97

Architektenburo L. Lafour en
R. Wijk bv · 216 dwellings and under-
ground car park, Witteneiland,
Jacob Catskade
  Designed in: 1993;
  with: Leen Borst, Jeroen Stins,
  Ingeborg van Lent, Gerard Laan;
  commissioned by: Bouwvereniging
  Rochdale, Amsterdam;
  realized by: Muwi van Gent's
  Bouwbedrijf, Amersfoort, 1996-97

Meyer en Van Schooten Architecten
B N A · 58 dwellings and 5 commercial
premises, Vespuccistraat/Bartholomeus
Diazstraat/Cabralstraat/Balbaostraat
  Designed in: 1992 & 1993;
  with: Arie van der Neut, Coen
  Kessels; *commissioned by:*
  Woningbouwvereniging Het Oosten,
  Amsterdam; *realized by:* Bouwbedrijf
  M.J. De Nijs en Zn bv,
  Warmenhuizen, 1994 & 1995

M V R D V (Winy Maas, Jacob van Rijs,
Nathalie de Vries) · Residential care
complex of 100 dwellings,
Ookmeerweg
  Designed in: 1994;
  with: Willem Timmer;
  commissioned by:
  Woningbouwvereniging Het Oosten,
  Amsterdam;
  realized by: Intervam-Noordwest bv,
  Almere/Amsterdam; Flevo
  Staalbouw, Hoorn, 1996-97

N S Ingenieursbureau (Rob Steenhuis) ·
N S traffic control building and technical
centre, De Ruyterkade
  Designed in: 1990;
  with: Marlies Janssen;
  commissioned by: N v Nederlandse
  Spoorwegen, Utrecht;
  realized by: Hollandse Beton
  Maatschappij bv, Amsterdam, 1994

Fenna Oorthuys · 8 dwellings, Kortrijk,
Nieuw Sloten
  Designed in: 1992;
  with: Yvonne van den Elsen;
  commissioned by: Wilma Vastgoed
  bv, Nieuwegein;
  realized by: Wilma Bouw bv,
  Amsterdam, 1995

O D 205 architectuur bv (Peter Defesche) · 61 apartments, offices, shops, and car park, Osdorpplein/Tussenmeer
> *Designed in:* 1994-95;
> *with:* Jan Hein Schouw;
> *commissioned by:* I N G Vastgoedontwikkeling bv, 's Gravenhage, Algemene Woningbouwvereniging, Amsterdam;
> *realized by:* Bouwcombinatie Osdorpplein (B A M Bredero Bouw, Amsterdam, B A M Woningbouw, Bunnik), 1996

Rowin Petersma, in collaboration with Liesbeth van der Pol · 31 dwellings, Quellijnstraat
> *Designed in:* 1993-94;
> *with:* Harald Advokaat, Mark Bangert, Bram Hoogendijk, Jan Andre Hoogland, Jan van der Schaaf, Sieto van der Scheer, Jolanda van der Sluis;
> *commissioned by:* Woningbouwvereniging de Dageraad, Amsterdam;
> *realized by:* Vink Bouw, Wevershoof, 1996

Tijmen Ploeg architect · Private house, Prinseneiland
> *Designed in:* 1993;
> *with:* Kurt Boomgaard;
> *commissioned by:* Lieven de Key in collaboration with occupants;
> *realized by:* Bouwbedrijf M.J. de Nijs & Zn bv, Warmenhuizen, 1994

Quist Wintermans Architekten bv (Paul Wintermans) · Cycle and pedestrian tunnels, Holtenbergweg/Burgemeester Stramanweg
> *Designed in:* 1994;
> *with:* Dirk Lohmeyer;
> *commissioned by:* Gemeentelijk Grondbedrijf Amsterdam;
> *realized by:* Bouwcombinatie Stadion, Amsterdam, Gebr. Beentjes, Uitgeest, Fa. Klaas Dekker, Warmerhuizen, 1996

Sjoerd Soeters Architecten bv · 151 dwellings, and 12 water side dwellings, Blankenbergestraat, Waregemstraat and surroundings
> *Designed in:* 1992;
> *with:* Dana Ponec, Erik van Oenen, Claudia Linders, Cobien Heuff, Ronno Stegeman, May Kooreman, Daniel Schneider;
> *commissioned by:* S F B/Bpf-bouw, Amsterdam; Wilma Vastgoed bv, Nieuwegein;
> *realized by:* Bontenbal Bouw, Reeuwijk, 1995

Steigenga Smit architekten · 24 dwellings, Vrolikstraat
> *Designed in:* 1994;
> *with:* Saskia van der Veen, Henk Uijtenhout, Gabriëlle van der Sleen;
> *commissioned by:* Woningbedrijf Amsterdam;
> *realized by:* B K Bouw, Bussum, 1996

Tangram Architekten bv · 79 dwellings
and 15 shops, Eerste van Swindenstraat
  Designed in: 1993;
  commissioned by: Woningbedrijf
  Amsterdam, Maarsen Bouw bv,
  Amstelveen, ABN AMRO
  Projectontwikkeling, Amsterdam;
  realized by: Maarsen Bouw bv,
  Amstelveen, Bouw- en
  Betontechniek, Amsterdam, 1996

René van Zuuk architecten · 'De
Toekomst', Ajax youth training centre,
stadium, Borchlandweg
  Designed in: 1995;
  commissioned by: AFC Ajax,
  Amsterdam;
  realized by: Bouwcombinatie
  Stadion, Amsterdam; 1996

Sources of illustrations

Aerophoto-Schiphol b.v.: pp. 32, 39, 120-121

Roos Aldershoff: pp. 22 (below), 102, 103 (above)

BouwWereld: p. 116

Jan Derwig: cover (housing Vespuccistraat) pp. 78, 79

dRO Amsterdam Vormgeving Fotobureau: p. 27

Frank van Epenhuysen: pp. 92, 93 (above), 128

Irene van Exel: pp. 118, 119

F & O Studio: p. 109

GVB Amsterdam Projectenbureau: p. 19 (below)

Maarten Kloos: pp. 105 (above), 125 (below)

Norbert van Onna: pp. 22 (above), 64, 65 (above), 89 (above)

Jeroen van Putten: pp. 62, 63

Wim Ruigrok: pp. 10, 16, 19 (above), 25, 26, 28, 35, 45, 47, 48, 49, 50, 51 (above), 52, 53 (below), 54, 58, 59 (above), 60, 61 (above), 67, 68, 72, 73, 75, 76, 80, 81, 82, 86, 87, 88, 95, 96, 100, 101, 104, 106, 107 (above), 108, 110, 115, 117, 124, 125 (above), 126, 127 (above), 133

Ger van der Vlugt: pp. 90, 91 (above), 122, 123

Illustrations not mentioned above have been supplied by the respective architects.

ARCAM *receives financial support from:*

Sector Ruimtelijke Ontwikkeling, Infrastructuur en Beheer,
    Gemeente Amsterdam
Dienst Welzijn, afdeling Kunst en Cultuur, Gemeente Amsterdam
Amsterdams Fonds voor de Kunst, Amsterdam
Stimuleringsfonds voor Architectuur, Rotterdam

ABN AMRO Projectontwikkeling, Amsterdam
G.W. Bakker Adviesgroep, Amsterdam
Ballast Nedam ProjectOntwikkeling, Rotterdam
Koninklijke BAM Groep, Bunnik
Bouwfonds Vastgoedontwikkeling, Hoevelaken
De Boer Den Hartog Hooft, Amsterdam
Breevast, Utrecht
Dura Bouwgroep, Rotterdam
Era Bouw, Zoetermeer
Heijmans Bouw en Vastgoedontwikkeling, Rosmalen
Hillen & Roosen Planontwikkeling, Amsterdam
Consortium IJ-DELTA, Amsterdam ZO
ING Vastgoed Ontwikkeling, Den Haag
Jones Lang Wootton, Amsterdam
Woonstichting De Key, Amsterdam
Van der Leij Groep, Amsterdam
MAB Groep, Den Haag
MUWI Vastgoed Ontwikkeling, Woerden
Bouwbedrijf M.J. de Nijs en Zn, Warmenhuizen
Woningbouwvereniging Het Oosten, Amsterdam
Oranje-Nassau Vastgoed (1997), Amsterdam ZO
Philips Pensioenfonds (1997), Eindhoven
PVF Pensioenen, Amsterdam
PVF Nederland, Amsterdam

Schiphol Vastgoed, Luchthaven Schiphol

SFB Vastgoed, Amsterdam

Smit's Bouwbedrijf, Beverwijk

Vermeer Grond en Wegen, Almere-De Vaart

Stichting Het Woningbedrijf Amsterdam, Amsterdam